Chopping My Row

Chopping My Row

Alma L. Jones

alma2011jones@gmail.com

ISBN-13: 9781546604495
ISBN-10: 1546604499

A Tribute to my mother, Lula Mae Peters Carr, Heart of My Heart

How Much, Momma

You will never know
Just how much
You'll miss her gentle,
Accepting touch
Until she has flown
Past time's clutch.

To Ernestine Scott for her friendship, enthusiasm, unwavering support, word-of-mouth push, and for doing a review of my book of poetry, *W.O.W. created w.o.w.*
To Ann Brown for her horticultural expertise and her friendship.
To Brenda McClerkin-Scott for her vigilance.
To Deborah Boyd for her love of people, expertise, push, and community spirit.
To Mitzi Morris for her wit and friendship.
To Sylvia Nance for her valued longtime friendship.
To the ladies' Bible group who asked me to do this book.
To Tomeka Perry for entrepreneurial support.
To my children, O'Brian and Candace.
TO MY FATHER, THE GOD OF HEAVEN, WHO MADE IT ALL POSSIBLE.

Contents

Introduction

§

PURPOSE: THE PURPOSE OF THIS book is to encourage ladies in their Christian walk, to emphasize our awesome task as mothers, grandmothers, sisters, aunts, cousins, and friends in the development of babes in Christ and the preparation of the future church. I hope these words can continue to speak to future generations long after I am gone.

Organization: This book uses the analogy of a vineyard or garden to describe a Christian life. I use a further analogy of chopping cotton on a row that has been assigned as a Christian's work for the Lord.

Scope: This book covers the period from when the Lord places a Christian to work in the field or vineyard to the judgment. I use storms as a way of discussing trouble in the Christian life, because nothing stops the work of a Christian faster than trouble or discouragement. I likened the storms to weeds that grow up on a typical row in a cotton field (as in tares among wheat). This book talks you through storms and then the possible purpose and results of them. The work strives to teach you to use your storms to the glory of God by blessing others with your reaction to your storms. It attempts to impress upon all readers the legacy being built daily in preparation for answering the roll one day. Christian actions and attitudes are stressed throughout the work.

The book is divided into thirteen lessons with subtitles under each. Each lesson includes narratives for the readers to work from to better portray the concept being taught or expressed. Questions to enhance the lesson are included also.

Note: Throughout this book, I have marked several phrases in green to remind you that as long as grass grows green from season to season, God is in control, and there is a reason for all that happens in our lives. We must use this knowledge to keep going—to keep stepping on.

Preface

§

LOOKING BACK ON MY LIFE, I can see so many things more clearly now. One of those things was the occasion for writing this book.

Was I surprised when I was asked to do a book for a ladies' Bible group? Yes, I was amazed—and I didn't think I could do it. Then I realized that it was the Lord utilizing me for His eternal purpose according to His plans. It still amazes me sometimes, the way He orchestrates His plans for us. He does it with such finesse, oftentimes without us even being aware of a particular pivotal point in our lives until several months or years later. He keeps me in awe, and I remain forever grateful for His grace in allowing this earthen vessel to work a while longer in His vineyard.

This book came about as follows. The Lord had blessed me when I published a volume of inspirational poetry, *W.O.W. created w.o.w.* A particular group of ladies loved the poetry so much that they wanted me to do a ladies' Bible class book for them. They used my motto, "Doing What I Can, While I Can," to motivate me, because as I just told you, I did not think I could do it.

If I were to diagram my life's work, centering it mainly around my writing for the Lord—including this book, *Chopping My Row*—it would look something like the following diagram.

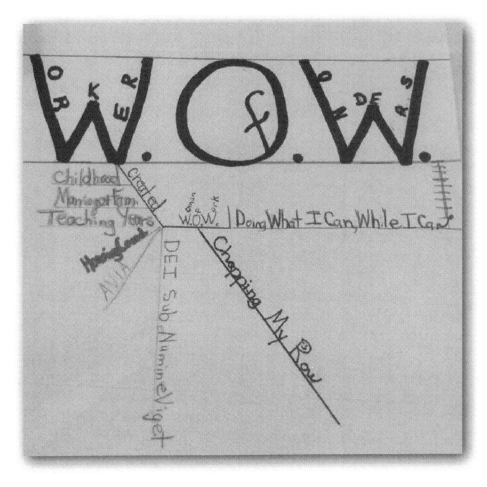

Prayer: Thank You for blessing me
In the writing of this book.
Thank You for blessing me
In the literary efforts that I undertook.
And for the words of encouragement
You let flow from my pen
So that I could use them for all women.

Life is a mystery, and sometimes only time will let you see.

Plan for Our Lives (Proverbs 19:21; Jeremiah 10:23 NKJ)

§

AIM: To BECOME MINDFUL OF the fact that our faithful Lord has a plan for our lives and to use that knowledge to deal with whatever comes our way. To realize that, though we may make plans for our life, ultimately it is not up to us; it is up to God.

Song: "Ultimately"

Because I know that He has a plan for my life, I can be happy. I can get immense pleasure from simple joys and simple gestures of love and care. I know, I know—I plead guilty to being a wearer of rose-tinted glasses.

Plans for Me

When I think about the fact
That You have plans for me,
It makes me want to run on
And be the best that I can be.

It makes me want to step high
And then step higher still.
It makes me want to encourage others
To get to know You and to always do Your will.

When I think about the fact
That You have plans for me,
I get a buoyancy in my step
That is easy for all to see.

And You know what? I don't care that they make
An example out of or make fun of me,
Because I am striving to please You, Jesus,
Whether through precipitous winds or calamity.

For I know to trust in You, no
Matter what comes my way,
Because I know that about what
Happens to me, You have the final say!
Psalm 5:11–12 NKJ
Proverbs 19:21 NKJ
(excerpt from *W.O.W. created w.o.w.*)

A Plan

God (my beginning)
Love (crafted in)
A Plan
Care packages (to sustain)
Love (gathered back with)
God (my ending)!
(excerpt from *W.O.W. created w.o.w.*)

This lesson aims to help us not become unduly bothered about things that change, because we know that, though we make plans, everything depends on the will of the Lord. That has not always been the case with me. I had to learn to expect change, because that is the way the Lord set things up. God does things per a plan, and according to Jeremiah 29:11 KJV, He has always had a plan for us. He put that plan for our lives in place a long time ago.

So, what exactly is a plan? A plan is a detailed method for achieving an end. It is a detailed formulation of a program of action. So to me, this means that God decided what would happen first in our lives, what would happen next, and so on and so forth. We know this is so because we were born, we grew up to become adults, we will grow old, and then we will die (Hebrews 9:27 NKJ).

That is the general plan for our lives. Change is built into the plan, because if it were not, we would stay babies. Now, we don't know the specifics that the Lord has put in place for our lives, but knowing that HE has a plan ought to give us, as His children, reassurance. We will talk about children in just a minute, but what I have said so far will help keep your faith in HIM strong.

How to Handle Unwelcome Change(s)

Now that we have established that change is inevitable, let's talk about some of the unpleasant things that happen in our lives. We have already stated that nothing lasts forever. Well, that applies to trouble too. It is just for a while. Though we do not know how long "a while" is, God does.

You remember the story of Job in the Bible, don't you? (Read Job 1:8–22 NKJ.) You can see from the reading that "Job was an upright man who feared God and eschewed evil." Job was trying to live for the Lord, so much so that the Lord bragged about him to Satan. Uh oh! And you know what Satan said? "No wonder! You have blessed everything that he has and all the works of his hands; what do you expect?" Now, those were not the exact words; I paraphrased and used today's language, but you get my drift.

Wonder why the story of Job was recorded in the Bible? The Lord made sure it was recorded in the Bible, His book, because HE knew that one day some of His children would need reassurance when they had to go through similar things in their lives. Thank You, Father, for looking through our lives before our time and placing things there that You knew we would need to make it through this land of our temporary dwelling.

Just as the Bible tells us how God's children's enemies caused them trouble, it has many episodes showing us that the Lord God took care of His people. And what we have to remember is that just as HE took care of them back then, because HE is faithful (1 Corinthians 1:9 NKJ), HE will take care of us now. We have to remember the other times in our lives when we have wrung our hands and cried to HIM, and HE brought us through. We must remember that HE took care of us in our mother's womb and has brought us on down to this present moment. In these plans that HE has made for us, there is help for the rough times that HE knows are coming. We must remember that in this storm, in this moment, HE is ever present and is working things out for our good (Romans 8:28 KJV).

Let's take a look at the story of Joseph in the Bible (Genesis 37:1–36 and chapters 39–41 NKJ). You see from this biblical account that Joseph experienced some unexpected, unpleasant changes in his life. He was thrown into a pit, sold to the Egyptians, and thrown into prison. We realize that these unwelcome changes were not things Joseph planned or enjoyed, but he managed to keep his faith in God. We can see the hand of the Lord working through whatever situations, traps, and pitfalls Joseph faced. When he was thrown into the pit, the Lord got him out of the pit, because if you will remember, it was his brothers' original intent to kill him and tell their father that a wild animal had slain him. That's what they thought they were going to do, but not so. The Lord already had a plan. He had the plan before Joseph was even born. Woo!

Ladies, when you think about it, you know that whatever moment we happen to be experiencing in our lives, whatever moment defines this moment or this day, God is already there working things out according to HIS plan! If you adopt this attitude in your life, you will have people marveling at your faith in God.

To get back to Joseph, the Lord had him find favor down in Egypt (care package- one of those tailor-made blessings with his name written all over it). He ended up in the house of an Egyptian nobleman who liked him very well. In that we can see the providential hand of the Lord working again. Uh oh! Not only did the nobleman like Joseph well enough, but apparently so did the nobleman's wife. Isn't that the way life seems to happen to us sometimes—you can't catch a break for anything! She meant to have Joseph one way or another, and when he would not sin against God by lying with her—but instead ran out of his coat to get away from her—she lied about him. And that lie caused poor Joseph to end up in prison. It seems that the adversary never leaves you alone if you are trying to live for the Lord. This was another unpleasant change for Joseph, but he kept his faith intact. How do we know? We know because references in the scripture let us know. Should I do this thing and sin against God? (Read Genesis 39:9 NKJ.)

We know that Joseph kept his faith in God throughout his entire ordeal, because in Genesis 50:20 he tells his brothers these beautiful words that bring music to my ears and joy to my soul every time I hear them: "You meant evil against me but God meant it for good to bring it about as it is this day." All in all, Joseph remained faithful until his death, as we can see from reading Genesis 50:24–25 NKJ.

Look

Look at what He has done
Through my poetry
He is bringing me to the place
Where He always intended me to be.
(Proverbs 19:21 NKJ)
(excerpt from *W.O.W. created w.o.w.*)

Trust Him to Work His Plan for You

And just as the Lord was with Joseph throughout the various setbacks in his life, so HE will be with us, too. (Read Genesis 39:2–6, 39:21–23, and 39:39–46 NKJ.) And just as He blessed Joseph, He will bless us, too.

So, ladies, don't be surprised to receive blessings when you stay faithful to God, for HE will "work things out for your good" (Romans 8:28 KJV). Start making some preparations for those blessings, if by doing nothing else but preparing yourself mentally.

I must confess, I have been blown away by the blessings I have received after some of my supercell storms ended. It gives further credence to that old song that says, "You can't beat God's giving, no matter how you try." I know that this song was written in reference to giving time, money, etc. to the Lord and His subsequent blessings, but I am speaking of what He has given mankind (His Son) and of the way He knows us so well that He can satisfy every fiber of our being! How swee-e-et it is to be loved by God! I just love being loved by Him, and I love trying to love Him back!

He has blessed me, y'all. He has blessed this lady who used to be a little nobody of a girl from Memphis, Tennessee. We will talk more about how He has blessed me in lesson 3.

He's Got a Plan!

So, if it feels as if you have been singled out by the world for persecution (more about persecution in lesson 9) or ridicule, don't worry about it. The Lord has picked you out according to His plan for you. And as we go through the lessons in this book, remember that the Lord has given you your row to chop, and though the cockleburs, Johnson grass, and morning glories tire you out, your Father sees you in your work (Hebrews 6:10 NKJ), for "His eyes are over the righteous and His ears open to their cry" (1 Peter 3:12 NKJ). When people single you out to fight with you, they are biting off more than they can chew. They can't handle a mouthful of God, because He cannot be bitten, period. He handles mankind Himself, according to His will! It is a fearful thing to fall into the hands of the Living God! I would not want to stir him up; would you?

He Made a Plan

HE looked upon her and chose
Her from the bustling pile.
He knew she would morph,
Though it would take her a while.

Forward I Go

Jeremiah 29:11 KJV has let me know
That You have already made plans
For me, and armed with that
Knowledge, it is forward that I go.

I see in nature when I look around
That you never leave situations to chance
For Your meticulous preparation
Can be seen throughout all creation.
You plan things down to minute details,

And because of that fact, I get assurance,
And armed with the knowledge of Your love,
It is on down the row that I go.

When I think about the fact that Your
Omnipotent hands fashioned me in my work
In the way that You wanted me to chop my row,
I get renewed vigor and tenacity
No matter what is thrown at me by my foe.
And it is with relish that I tell the world
My God loves you and me, and this is a
Fact that I know.
For knowing that I am a part of His eternal plan,
I chop the weeds that are on my row
Whether they are tall or high.
It is with determined tenacity
That I, with my eyes on my Father, work my row,
As toward the eternal city I go.

Still Rising Despite the Heavy Weights

Hard Blows the Gale

Hard blows the gale,
For it's a mighty storm
To buffet the person of faith
To become his or her norm,
To make a person of
Muscles with rare form.
James 1:3 NKJ

§

Didn't Count on That

You don't count on
Being left alone so that
It can be seen
What's in your heart,
Yet God did Hezekiah that way,
Like things may be done today.
2 Chronicles 32:31 NASB

Somebody once said, "Faith is not faith until it is put to the test." That is so true, and to that I would like to add an Almaism:

"The size of your faith determines the size of your test."

§

DISCUSSION QUESTIONS
1. How does Proverbs 19:2 NKJV 1 apply to us today?

_____

2. Name two scriptures that say that the Lord has a plan for our lives.

_____

3. Does Romans 8:28 KJV NKJV mean that nothing bad will ever happen to us? Explain.

_____

4. According to Jeremiah 9:24 NKJ NKJV, how does God feel about us bragging?

_____

5. How does having a strong faith benefit us?

_____

6. Read 1 Peter 3:12 NKJV and Hebrew 6:10 NKJV.
7. In 2 Chronicles 32:31 NKJV, why does God leave Hezekiah alone? Do things like this happen today?

For Further Reading
Jeremiah 29:11 KJV NKJV

Storms (Isaiah 41:13 NKJV)

§

AIM: To REALIZE THAT THOUGH trouble and trials are a part of the Christian life, we are never alone. To learn how to handle times of adversity.

Song: "Shelter in the Time of a Storm"

Sometimes we have to go through some rough things in life, either things we bring on ourselves or things that people cause to happen to us. At times we can be so beaten down that it is hard to keep the upbeat feeling that we started off with, huh? Well, we are going to be dealing with storms in this lesson, but I want to begin by saying a couple of things to you:

1. You must never think that giving your heart and soul to the Lord means that the adversary is going to stop bothering you. Nothing could be further from the truth. Remember Job.
2. The second thing to remember is to give all your problems to Him, and don't pick them back up again. This is covered in more detail in lesson 8.

Now, let's work through storms and how to handle them, shall we? As soon as something we don't like or don't understand happens in our lives, most of us question the Lord: "Is He listening? Can He hear me? Does He care?" Y'all know how we do sometimes. But what we need to remember is that sometimes the adversary uses storms to weaken our faith. Haven't you ever noticed how many times the adversary kicks us when we are down? He does that because he knows that if we believe the Lord no longer hears us, we will cease to pray, thereby damaging our relationship with God. So he will go after us just like he did Job. You see, when you are committed to God as Job was, the adversary knows it.

The adversary figures that if he can get the "Job" in the church, he can get the rest of us. It seems as if every time you get your head above water, something else happens, and you are right back where you started. Never forget that God is omnipotent; nothing happens without His permission (Job 1:12; Lamentations 3:37–38 NKJV), and nothing surprises or confuses Him. When we have setbacks, we must remember that they are temporary. After all, "All things work together for good for those that love the Lord" (Romans 8:28 KJV NKJV).

In lesson 1 we learned that the Lord has a plan for our lives. Well, use that piece of information to keep you strong. This God you are questioning now is the same God that brought you through your yesterdays. This same God is the One of whom the disciples asked, "What manner of man is this that even the wind and sea obey Him?" (Matthew 8:27 KJV)

Mark Your Storm in Green

I have marked the above phrase in green
To remind you that as long as grass grows
Green from season to season,
God is in control and there is a reason
For the turmoil in your life, because He plans
Things out to, in a simultaneous way,
Benefit you and some other woman or man.

Just like a teacher crafts a lesson for her students
With a primary objective in mind,
She always remembers other concepts
That have not been mastered by the kids yet
And builds, within the lesson, supplementary
Exercises to strengthen any remaining weaknesses
That the lesson might find.

That being said, you know that the Lord
Is the Master Teacher, for sure,
So realize that anything that He has you go through
Is according to His masterful plan to
Bless and effect some needed cure.

THE ADVERSARY HAS CHOSEN YOU

What do you do when you figure out that the adversary has chosen you for an onslaught? You have to stick close to the Lord at all times. This means that when your troubles come at you all at once and you have to contend with two years' worth of trouble within a few months, you talk to God more than ever! This may be one of those times when even your friends get tired of trying to lift you up, just as Job's friends got tired. But you must keep going! If you have the presence of mind to realize that what is happening to you is just not normal, then have the presence of mind to know that there is a Supreme Supernatural Force that no one and nothing can get the best of. Just remember that He sees, He cares, He is on the job, and He never rests from protecting His children.

Standing on the Top of the Mountain

Standing on the top of the mountain feeling blessed,
Standing on the top of the mountain feeling no stress,
Fell from the mountaintop to the valley

And couldn't see the light of day.
But, you know what?
Carried Jesus with me every step of the way!

§

Strength Gone

I'm glad that His love covers me
In all my weakness and my trials,
For when my strength is tried and gone,
His strengthening power takes hold and carries me on.

§

Weed Problems on the Row

Back in lesson 1, we talked about some of the weeds you can run into when chopping a row of cotton, namely cockleburs, morning glories, and Johnson grass. I chose the metaphor of cotton chopping because I did a little of it as a child, and I remember how tiresome and tedious it could be. Even when I finally learned how to chop cotton properly, I still was not very good at it, because in order to be good at it, you had to have a keen eye for spotting the morning-glory vines that grew in with the cotton. If you did not cut off the vines at ground level, they would grow all tangled and entwined in the cotton, stunting its growth. I learned that cutting them off at the ground stopped their spread, and they would die and choke the cotton no longer.

Then there was the problem of cockleburs which are pictured above. I learned to chop them down when they were young and toss them in the row middle (space between the rows), where they caused no

more trouble. I learned quickly not to get entangled in the cockle-burs, because they stuck anyplace they could and were quite painful to get out of clothing and hair.

Oh, but what about that Johnson grass? That stuff was a hot mess to deal, with, as my friend Mitzi would say. We were always told to dig Johnson grass up by the root. Let's take this grass and break down the trouble it caused in a row, shall we? The Johnson grass would stunt the growth of the cotton plant, so it had to be removed. When I use Johnson grass in the metaphor of Christians trying to work on a row in the Lord's vineyard, doing what they have been given to do in this Christian life, I liken it to when a supercell storm hits our life. Above, when I mentioned being faced with two years' worth of trouble in a matter of months, that is analogous to encountering Johnson grass. This definition of the grass illustrates why farmers detest it so much: "Perennial with vigorous rhizomes. Coarse, rapidly growing, difficult to control grass that reaches up to 2 m tall. Plants can rapidly develop colonies. Johnson grass, considered one of the 10 most noxious weeds in the world, is especially troublesome in cotton fields. Infestations of the grass in crops, because it is competitive with them, can reduce harvest yields significantly" (<http://www.texasinvasives.org/plant_database/ Texas Invasives).

I remember a few lessons about dealing with Johnson grass in my youth that can apply to figuratively chopping a row in the Christian life.

1. The first step is to make sure your hoe is sharpened to the max. (Make sure that you are prayed up.)
2. Make sure you eat a good lunch. (Make sure that you are read up in your Bible.)
3. Get some extra help with chopping the grass. (Find prayer partners to help you make it through the storms, because

the Bible says, "The prayers of the righteous availeth much" [James 5:16 KJV)

4. Be prepared for your muscles to be sore when you get through the patch. (Be prepared for the "Why me?" blues to settle in.)
5. Rub in some liniment as necessary. (Worship services will soothe the battered muscles of your faith.)

If you are battling a particularly nasty storm right now, allow me to say that I know you feel like it's going to kill you; I did too as you will see when you reach page 40. I know you feel like you can't take it; I did too. I know you feel like this will make you crazy; I thought so too. Often, I had to cry the way I saw my mother do when I was a little girl. There have been times during prayer when I have had tears sliding down my face as I talked to my Father. But through it all, though I wrung my hands, though I cried and prayed, I kept my faith. As a matter of fact, usually by the end of my prayer, my faith had kicked up to its highest level (ramrod strong). I began to wait on the Lord. I read my Bible daily, and I waited and prayed on a continuous basis (Psalm 27:14 and Isaiah 40:31). So, too, you must endure. Your breakthrough/anointing is on the other side of the trouble you are walking or crawling through. Your only way out is to go through it.

Remember the poem above that gave you stepping-on power when it told you to paint your storms green. And then, sister, you step on anyway!

NOWHERE TO RUN

Sometimes in our battle to be a good soldier for the Lord, we come to the intersection of two streets called Nowhere to Run and Nowhere to Hide. Remember the fact that David had to run and then had to hide in a cave to keep Saul from killing him (1 Samuel 22:1 NKJV). Then you think about Jesus and remember that He said that "He is going to wipe all of our tears away" (Revelation 21:4) when we get home. That's one thing that we have to remember; all we have to do is make it home. Then we think about the times the Lord has brought us through before. It will help us to remember the words of that old song that says, "All that I am and ever hope to be, I owe it all to Thee." That means that all that I am, claim to be, and am *gonna* be is because of the Lord. The two preceding sentences should refer our minds back to the plan that the Lord has for our lives (Lesson 1, Jeremiah 29:11 KJV; Psalm 37:23; Proverbs 16:9; 1 Corinthians 2:9 NKJV).

People Are Watching Me
Battle Scars

Have gained some battle scars
In my skirmishes with the adversary
But would do it all again
If told, though of the enemy I'm wary.
(excerpt from *Excelsior*)

Think You Can't Make It

So, you think you cannot make it.
I tell you that is just not so.
Listen to me, sister of mine,
And I'll tell you what I know.

Let me tell you a little story about something that happened in my life.

On April 16, 1987, my house burned down. The fire was so hot that it even burned up the floor. If you have never experienced a house fire, you have no true idea of the trauma it wreaks on your life. It will attack you in ways you never even thought about. It will shake your faith to the core. You will find that you miss things you had previously taken for granted, such as your children's baby pictures. You will think about them and cry. But then you will remember the scripture Job 14:14 NKJV.

Remember when I told you to always look for your blessing in your storm? Mmm hmm.

Job 14:14 NKJV is a good reference scripture for that. Read it. Start thinking about *what possible good* can come out of the chaos or trouble in which you find yourself.

Below are some blessings that came from my house fire, some of which I realized then; other realizations came years later.

1.   There was no loss of life in the fire. At the time of the fire, my babies were at school, my husband was at work, and I was in my classroom teaching.
2.   My mother, bless her heart, was in her own house next door at the time of the fire, which engulfed both homes. The tip end of one of her plaits burned off—and that is all. When I got home that day, she was standing across the road from the blazing house, along with some of the other neighbors, looking dazed, as if she could not believe this had happened. The fire had already burned her house to the ground and was well on its way to devouring mine. But she was okay! I got to have my momma for seventeen more blessed years. When she did die, I realized what the Lord had not allowed the fire to take from me that April day. (Her leaving me is a narrative for another time, but suffice it to say that I did not know anything could hurt that badly.)

3. Our cat's paws got scorched, and it had to spend a couple of days at the vet, but it was okay too. It lived to a ripe old life after the fire.

4. I vowed that if I ever got any more china, I would use it regularly and not leave it sitting up in the china cabinet waiting for some special occasion.

5. I cried a lot over the lost pictures of my kids, but various family members and friends brought me copies that I had given to them.

6. We had no insurance at the time, but these days we are insurance poor!

7. We have had several riding mowers since losing the brand new one we had used all of our income tax refund on to buy that had burned up in the fire. It was less than a week old, too! Ouch!

8. The kids' schools supplied them with new bikes and clothes.

9. My school took care of my clothes, kitchenware and replaced a precious broom I cried so much over. As a matter of fact, I received three brooms!

10. Church members, black and white (there's a lesson in that for us today), supplied everything else—and I do mean everything else. It was common for someone to walk up to me and ask what else I needed or to shake my hand and leave it graced with a $100 bill. I still have a mental picture of three church members bringing a brand new couch and armchair into my house. I never knew people could care that much. That outpouring of love across racial barriers put a smile on my face. I think it was God's way of sending me a care package—one of those tailor-made blessings with my name written all over it (more about this in lesson 8). I have never forgotten the feeling of receiving the gift. I also have never forgotten that people will watch you to see how you handle your adversity—and your reaction to your own storm might just be a blessing for somebody with a storm headed their way.

11. We stayed with my husband, Paul's aunt and uncle for two nights after the fire and then moved to a little yellow house on a hill in the heart of Martin. It even had a washing machine—not as nice as the one I had, but a washing machine nevertheless.
12. My mother was given her own apartment, for which she was very thankful.
13. This experience taught me that people will look at you to see how you handle a situation in your times of stress. I repeated this item because I want you to be very aware of it. Our reactions do speak for or against the Lord.

Must Remember

Must remember that people are watching me
As I travel along life's highway.
Must remember that I might influence someone
By what I do and what I say.

Earlier, I told you about a lady who complimented me because my faith stayed strong during the time of my fire—you know, losing so much, and no insurance to boot. She thought it was outstanding that I could have a smile on my face during that time. She told me she wished she had a faith that strong. I thanked her and kept moving. Well, about seven to eight months later, this same lady was diagnosed with stage-four cancer. She lived less than a year after her diagnosis.

She told me something I will remember as long as the Lord allows my thought processes to flow: "Alma, come here a minute, I want to talk to you," she said to me one day. "I just wanted to tell you, Alma, that I admire you. Yes, I know that shocks you, but I do. This is why I admire you. Back in the spring, when your house burned, you kept a smile on your face. And now I can have that same strong faith that you displayed. That is how I am making it through this cancer and the ravages it has put my life and my body through. So Alma, I just wanted to say thank you."

Folks, I have never forgotten the lesson she taught me that day, even though she did not realize she was teaching me one. And that is why you will often hear me say, "Be a blessing to others in their storm, even though you are going through storms of your own—because, ladies, we just don't know why we are going through what we go through."

14. Several years after my house fire, one of the teachers at my new school (had moved to a different job in a regular classroom in a different school after so many years of praying) lost her home to a fire. Since the school where I was moved was the one that had bought new clothes and a bike for my son, they knew that I had suffered a fire a few years back. Therefore, they came to me with a request that I list some things the teacher would need after a fire. I listed what I thought was needed, and I reiterated, again and again, the need to take her a broom. Most everyone scoffed at the idea and would not do it. They took all kinds of things, big and little. When they got to her she was overwhelmed with gratitude, but she burst out crying, saying, guess what? You got it: "But I don't even have a broom!" They sent some of the men pronto to get that broom, along with a mop and dustpan, etc. They all said, "Alma told us to get a broom!" Now, here is the point I wanted to make with the broom scenario. If I had never experienced a house fire, I would not have known the absolute lostness, the sense of floundering you feel and the necessity of bringing a broom to the victim of the fire. That fire taught me how to be empathetic in a way I would not have been had I not suffered a house fire of my own.

15. This experience taught me that "All things work together for good for those that love the Lord" (Romans 8:28 NKJV). Though the fire was not a comfortable or enjoyable experience for me, it taught me to lean on the Lord in a way that I never had. I had always been close to the Lord and knew it, or so I thought, but this fire taught me a level of dependence on faith that I had never known. And it taught me a vulnerability I had not had since becoming an adult.

Be a blessing to someone else in their storm, even though you are going through storms of your own.

ULTIMATELY

Ultimately. What a word! What a word! What does this word mean, and why am I so fascinated by it? Just hold your horses, and I will tell you why I love this word so much. I hope that when I finish my explanation you will feel the same way about it. The word ultimate is defined as *maximum, final,* or *supreme.* I like to say that it refers to a time "When all has been said and all has been done—the buck stops here." Now, I want you to hold onto that thought for me, because I am going someplace with it. I'll be there in a minute or so. All I ask you to do for me is this: if, at the end of this lesson, your load has been lightened or if you have been given a better perspective on handling stressful situations, then pass the blessing on to somebody else. That's all I ask, okay? All right, here we go!

I was not there when "the foundation of the earth was laid, its measurements were set, its bases were sunk and its cornerstone laid. I was not there when the morning stars sang together and all the sons of God shouted for joy" (Job 38). I am not going to take the time to cite the entire chapter here, but you would do well to revisit it if you haven't read it lately. Whenever I am going through trying times in my life, I read that passage, and then I talk to my Father, and this is the gist of what I say to Him:

Owing to your faithfulness, Father, I know that everything in my life is going to be okay, because you have already told me so in your word. I have just finished reading from the book of Job 38 NKJV, so I repent, Father, for the times, as now, that I think, 'This isn't fair, what's happening to me. But I didn't do anything.' I am so sorry and ask You to forgive me. You see, Father, I *forgot to remember* that though it is hard right now, it is still not the charcoal-bucket days *(days in the dead of winter that our lights, gas and water had been disconnected because my mother did not have the money to pay it)*—that, ultimately, You have control of everything that happens in my life. I also know that when Job was going through his trials, nothing could happen to him without Your say-so. You limited how much the adversary could do to him, just as you limit how much turmoil the adversary can inflict upon me. I also know that You brought Job through okay. But you didn't stop there. Just as a mother prepares for a new baby, in all Your wisdom You created hope for me when You had Job's story recorded. You have shown Your love in everything You have done for us, especially through Your Son, Jesus.

You not only had the Bible written for us, but you made sure scripture told us that the Bible contains "Everything that pertains to life and Godliness." And then you had it further say that "Whatsoever things that were written before time were written for our learning." (Romans 15:4 KJV) It is no coincidence the Bible contains examples and stories for us that we turn to often for encouragement and spiritual nourishment. After all, You had the Bible prepared for us with love. I am proud to be living during the time of free Bible reading and in a country where there is no penalty of death for exercising our right to serve You.

A prayer for the journey so far: Thank You, Father, and forgive me when I complain about the storms in my life. I will keep reminding myself of all of the preparations that you have made for me, and I will keep saying, "I don't believe You brought me this far to leave me."

DON'T BECOME DISCOURAGED

We talked about finding the blessing in your storm to keep you from becoming discouraged. God sees your pain, your confusion, and your dwindling faith. You have to think that living the Christian life is not all about you. It is about your faith in God and what you are willing to give up for Him.

When Your Load Gets Heavy

When your load gets heavy,
When your feet get worn,
When your soul gets weary,
When your eyes get tired
Of shedding tears because
Of darts that have been fired
And the muck of life in which
You find yourself mired,
Keep stepping, in Jesus's name.
Remember, He sees; He knows; He cares,
And only "mustard seed" faith is required!

I want to talk to you briefly about three things: skipping faith, tottering faith, and "ultimately" faith. Here is an explanation of each, as I see things:

* Skipping faith is the kind of faith I had as a child, when I skipped with joy quite a bit. That is why I choose to call my

childhood faith *skipping faith*. This kind of faith propelled me onward through my charcoal-bucket, cotton-chopping, water-hauling, holey-shoes days. This was the faith that told me I was just as good as the next person, because the Lord loved me. This was the faith that told me I could and would be somebody one day if I just kept on believing in Jesus.

- Tottering faith is the kind that I gained as a result of life happening to me without the full benefit of the Lord's protection—in other words, when the hedges were taken down and I learned a smidgen of what life was about without that protection I had thought I would never lose. I remember thinking, beforehand, "What would I do if I ever lost this protective help that is such an integral part of my life?" Another name for this type of faith is crawling faith. In this stage of faith, you learn just how helpless you are without Him, but you keep moving toward Him, even when you have to crawl.

- "Ultimately" faith is that kind of faith that has seen hardships and knows what the loss of the protective hedges can do to a life. This is the kind of faith that says, "One day, He's going to wipe all of my tears away if I just remain faithful and keep moving toward Him and Heaven, my home." This is the stage when we tearfully rejoice because the hedges have been put back in place, and a battle-scarred and weary soldier can have her wounds tended.

This is my walk of faith, y'all. This came to me in a moment of epiphany as I was saying my morning prayer. I hope it blessed your spirit in whatever way you needed it to, today. I make no apologies. This is who I am.

Note: I do know that *ultimately* is an adverb and that I am using it incorrectly in bullet three. But using it this way epitomizes what the word does for me. It says to me, though things are happening and have happened in my life that I just do not understand, God does.

Words that end in "-ly" tell how and to what degree something is done. Adverbs are used to modify a verb, an adjective, or another adverb and are often used to show degree, manner, place, or time. When I see this word or hear it, it says to me that the Master Planner has everything under control. Because of His meticulous planning for my life, He has "jic's" (just-in-case's) in place for all contingencies; He has care packages available for me and messengers ready to deliver them to me according to all of the "-ly's" in my life.

Ultimately

As a young person, when
I first went to college,
I knew what my life was about.
I knew what I wanted to be.
I had my life plans all laid out.

I knew the number of kids
That I would someday have.
I knew the type of home
That I would someday buy,
For I had grabbed life by the tail,
And I was reaching for the sky.

What I didn't realize was
That it was not all about me.
It was about my life PLANNER,
The God of all eternity.

When I wanted to go left
But had to go right,
I shrugged off the inconvenience
And kept my well-laid-out
Plans within my sight.

When I tripped and fell
While running my race,
I picked myself up, dusted
My knees, and wiped my face.

I kept skipping along,
Though I had to hobble now and again.
I kept moving toward my dreams,
Though sometimes I was too winded
To sing my song.

By the time I had climbed
A few mountains and labored up some hills,
I began to wonder to myself,
"Hey! Wonder what's up; what gives?
For this is not the type of life
That I had planned to live."

Then I thought about Jonah
From the Bible days,
Who had not wanted to do
God's bidding, who wanted to follow
His own ways.

But that was Jonah, and
I am me.
Besides, the God of the Bible
Does not have special plans for me.

HE deals with superstars like David,
Daniel, Elijah, and the Hebrew Boys.
He does not bother with folk like you and me,
Who have always been free to do
Whatever we enjoyed.

Then why are all these things
Happening to me?
An elderly neighbor said to me one day,
"You are not your own boss.
Jesus has the final say.

"Plans were made for you
Way before you were born
You have to take your faith in your hand
And begin your God-planned sojourn.

"You see, Jeremiah 29:11 KJV says that
The LORD does have plans for you.
So, baby girl, just you wait and
See where HE leads you to."

Yes ultimately, HE has the final say.
I'm just glad that HE gives us time
To change our planned route
According to what HIS plans say.

Though this day be filled with
Chaos and storms,
I know that this page is but one
From the plan book that was
Written before I was born.

So, I'll not worry about what's coming ahead,
Because just like the lilies of the field
And the sparrows of the air,
HE has always kept me clothed
And has always kept me fed.

I'll just lean on HIM, because ultimately
HE cares for me; I know
Because HE finished this story
Of mine a long time ago.

Ultimately, ultimately—
What a word; what a word.
One of the most beautiful words that
I have ever heard.

So, I would not change one step of
My journey, as I found the path for my life.
I'll just hold on to "ultimately" and say...

🎶 "Ultimately, oh-h-h ultimately
Ultimately, oh-h-h ultimately
God has a plan, a plan for me
And the name of that plan, I call 'Ultimately.'" 🎶
(excerpt from *W.O.W. created w.o.w.*)

When I wrote the poem above, it had such an impact upon my life that I made a song out of it! I wanted the masses to praise Him and get enjoyment and encouragement from the words, too.

If it has not already been released to YouTube, it will be shortly. I thank God for giving us the gift of song so that we can sing our cares away and offer praise to Him at the same time.

Aside: God finds superstars among common folk. Just sayin'—you never know the reason behind your storm.

Let's always be mindful of the fact that when we go through things that we think are just horrible, they may actually be the avenue to our blessings. Remember Abraham (Genesis 22:9–13, 17 NKJV).

Also, Paul and Silas used songs to help them through their storm of being imprisoned (Acts 16:25–34 NKJV).

Yesterday, the singing took my joy to soulful new heights. There is something about singing that lifts our spirits faster than most anything can. I agree with the psalmist, who said in Psalm 81:1, "Sing aloud unto God our strength: make a joyful noise unto the God of Jacob; I will sing of the mercies of the Lord forever: with my mouth will I make known thy faithfulness to all generations" (89:1 KJV) and "O come, let us sing unto the LORD: let us make a joyful noise to the rock of our salvation" (Psalm 95:1 NKJV).

When you put your heart into your singing, a contagion of joy seeps from your soul and soars through the air, enrapturing all who are present. I hope your worship was as uplifting as the one I was a part of yesterday. We had a hallelujah good time and gave God some praise.

Earlier, I talked to you about the other side of "through." When it's over—when it is all over—then the celebration will begin. And you will celebrate! I know; been there, done that.

Yes, storms will come from time to time, with various intensity levels. But think about this: remember Job in the Bible? The worst part of his storms was the last part. That, my friend, lets you know that you must be close to "the other side of through" (i.e., your storm being over). Another way to say this is, "It's always darkest before the dawn."

So tell yourself, "I can and will make it, because I trust Him to lead me to the 'other side of through.'"

> If you wait, come what may,
> You will have a brighter day,
> For no storm lasts always.

Just lean on His plans for you,
And He will make a way.

Discussion Questions

1. Why was the book of Job written?

_____

2. Does the adversary know who is the most committed to God?

_____

3. Do you believe that you can be hit by a storm, be blessed yourself, and help someone else at the same time?

_____

4. Are God's people ever in fear for their lives because of serving Him? (1 Samuel 22:1 NKJV)

_____

5. God used a burning bush to gain Moses's attention, and He made the winds and water bend to His will and got the disciples' attention. Does He use measures like that today?

_____

For Further Reading

Psalm 27:14, Isaiah 40:31, Romans 5:3–5, Psalm 5:11–12, Romans 5:35, Job 23:10, 1 Peter 1:7–17 NKJV

The Other Side of Through (Job 42:10-12 KJV)

§

AIM: To LEARN THAT THERE are blessings in our storms if we persevere. To further realize that storms change us.

Song: "One More Sunny Day"

Track Record

Look at His track record.
It's plain for all to see.
He had it put in His Bible
That He had scholars write
For you and for me!

Look at His track record
From church folks that you know.
Look at His track record
Everywhere you go.

Look at His track record
Of what He has done for you.
Remember all the "stuff"
That He brought you "to" and "through!"

Now that your storm is over, be prepared to tell others how you made it. You should be saying to yourself, "I am ready to work for Him now." Why? Well, just as a physical storm may do some damage to crops and vegetation, it makes the remaining vegetation grow profusely. By the same token, you will be so thankful your storm is over that you will want to thank Him, and you will change in whatever ways it takes to avoid a repeat performance. I can tell you a few things about making it through your storm, because I have been through some myself.

If you are still in your storm, whatever you do, don't give up. You see, if I had never experienced any storms, I could not tell you that the Lord will make a way. I could not stand here and smile through the pages of my book when I talk about how He delivered me. I could not tell you with conviction, as my Gran Gran, Sister S. E. Hampton, late of Milan, Tennessee, used to say, "I declare He will make it all right."

What better person to comfort you when the bottom falls out of your life than one whose bottom has already fallen out? This person can comfort you in a way nobody else can. The fact that the Lord brought this person through underscores the fact that He is able to bring you through, too.

I told you in the preceding paragraph that my storm changed me. Let me tell you how. I found out I was not as strong as I thought I was. Like Job, I came to a fuller understanding of the God that we serve. Like Job, I realized that I had to trust Him, though I didn't understand. I realized that when I wanted to talk with Him so I could understand, in a way I was asking, "Why?" I was, in a way, saying that I thought what was happening to me was not fair. But oh, when I read the first verse in the fortieth chapter of Job, I realized that if I never understood the whys and wherefores of my journey, I had better trust Him and keep stepping for Him. (Read Job 40:1 KJV.)

That verse says, and I am paraphrasing, "Oh! So, you, fault finder, are going to contend with God Almighty so that you can be justified? Can the thing that was created correct the Creator?" Folks, after I read Job, chapters 40–42 KJV, I lay my own hand over the mouth of my mind and said no more about wondering why. I just kept asking for forgiveness, and I kept stepping, and I kept saying, "Whatever is the Lord's will." My mind focused on the fact that God was dealing with me, and I did as Isaiah said, "I will wait for my change to come." (Job 14:14 KJV) I told myself again, "Alma, 'Wait, I say, on the Lord'" (Psalm 27:14 KJV).

So, if you are in the midst of a storm and you feel like crying, it's okay. You wouldn't be human if you didn't cry when you hurt. But don't forget to pray while you are crying, and sometimes even afterward. But here's the ticket: cry only for so long, and then remember Whose child you are. Give whatever problem that is bothering you to Him, and wait to see how He delivers you. There is a song by the Canton Spirituals that speaks to my soul in times like these: "Watch Him Move."

Why am I including so much about storms in this book? I will tell you why. Nothing else affects a Christian's relationship to the Lord in a negative way like trouble. I don't care what kind of trouble you might have; it works on your faith. Poor health, financial problems, grief, etc.—they affect us all. But I will tell you one thing: when you do get out of your storm, your relief will be so great that some of you will practically run to tell your story. Others of you will at least reach over and help others through their storm by telling of yours.

Continuing my treatise on storms, at times in my life when I have been at my wit's end, God has stepped right on in through my trials, through my situations, through my adversities, and through my enemies and rescued me. He has picked me up numerous times, and I cannot but believe that He is still mindful of me now! That is what you have to hold onto. We do not need to "Fear the one who can destroy the body but the One Who can destroy body and soul in hell" (Matthew 10:28).

So, if there are those among my readers who are enduring seemingly impossible situations, I am writing to tell you not to worry and not to be so stirred up in your spirit that it hurts down to the depths of your soul and works on weakening your faith. Why? Because I serve a God who is faithful, and He always—I mean *always*—has His eyes over the righteous and His ears open to their cry. He has walked me through some fiery furnaces in my life, folks. So, I keep stepping! As the old folks used to say, "I've come too far with Him, and I ain't gon' turn around now!"

Those of you who are reading this book and have something heavy on your heart, take heart. Learn all you can from your situation. You know why? Because sometimes we are called upon to speak to people who are carrying a heavy burden. The Lord may have orchestrated the circumstances of life so that you are the only one who can help them, the only one they will listen to. Just tell yourself, "If this is one of the ways HE is using me to work for HIM, if this is some of the Johnson grass on my row, then that's okay." But remember, too, that He has you learning lessons from your storms. I plan to work for HIM until HE calls me home. I'm not worried much about me now, because as I read in my devotional book this morning and yesterday morning, I can do and I can go because **He is!**

A Light at the End of the Tunnel
So you see a light at the end of the tunnel and have ascertained that it is not a train. Good! That means things are finally turning around for you. No more valleys to scale, no more rivers to cross. For right now, anyway! Isn't it a great feeling? Enjoy! The Bible says rejoice, so have at it!

Now a word of caution:

There's a Reason

Remember the valleys that you've been through
That there was always a reason for them.
Remember to lend a tender ear and a helping hand
When you see someone's faith wane and their
Christian light begin to go dim.

Remember the tender words of comfort
That were spoken and written to you.
Extend likewise a message of hope
To your fellowman whose trials are not yet through!

PEACE TIMES

What you do during storms and in peacetime, too, prepares you for your next storm, because, whether we realize it or not, we are always in one of three states with storms: either we just got out of one, are in the midst of one, or are getting ready to go into one. With that in mind, here's what I do:

First, I do a morning meditation and prayer.

The next thing I do is determine that I am going to be cordial and kind to people I meet. Why do I do this? I don't know why I started this. It is something I have done all my life. I know two things about this practice of mine:

1) It makes me feel good.
2) I discovered several years ago a passage in the Bible that has resonated with me ever since. That passage is Isaiah 50:4 MSG. Read it. Basically, the passage says that if you have the

gift of being an encourager, it did not come to you by mere chance. It says that, that gift is to be used to help your fellowman, who may be weary from time to time. This is a gift I have been given, and I use it to the glory of God. All that is to say that I am a caring person by nature. People seem to want to tell me their problems, and I listen. Why? Because it is part of my makeup and part of my life's journey to "Do What I Can, While I Can." (And too, remember that scripture that says, "Have entertained angels unawares" [Hebrews 13:2 KJV].)

You will find that thinking positively will help you change your attitude and be able to encourage others. At any rate, this works well for me. I hope you will try it and it works well for you as you develop your ministry, things you do to and for the glory of God.

OTHER BLESSINGS DURING AND AFTER THE STORM

We have talked about the Lord having plans for our lives, right? Well, allow me to delve into my life plan a bit. When I was a little girl, I used to ask the Lord every day for wisdom. Why? I did this because we were taught that Solomon did this, and I wanted to be blessed like that, too. I asked for wisdom every day without fail. When I look back on my life, I can see that the Lord heard and answered my prayers. I noticed it some: in my classwork as a child or in the way I tried to help Momma work some problem out or figure out the meals for the week.

But folks, when I look back on my life now, I can see what the Lord has done for me.

- My Learning Days *(Developing My Skills)*: I already told you that I asked for wisdom as a child daily. But here is something else I was good at as a child: writing stories. I entertained my friends with my stories and ended some of them with a question about what happened next. Let me tell you, my stories created no small stir in our fourth-grade classroom! Now, after a successful teaching career, I find myself going back to my childhood pastime of writing. This time I write about all sorts of things, but the most important thing I write about is HIM.

- My Teaching Days *(Instructor in Others' Learning):* Even as a child, I have always been good at explaining complex things in a simple manner. I remember on one occasion my teacher was trying to explain something to one of my classmates. He just could not get it, so she suggested that I try to explain it to him. I did, and he got it! She used me quite a bit that year for peer tutoring. Of course, they didn't call it that back then, but you get my point. Don't you see? God was building in me the tools to be a teacher? Yep, that is what I ended up doing for a living.

- My Writing Days *(Recording Life Experiences and Words of Wisdom for Future Generations):* I have learned to carry my own books with me at all times. I never let myself go anyplace without some copies of my books. I am out of poetess/author cards; I cannot seem to keep them long. And get this: I have written this book for you about the way I'm trying to live my life for Him, and one of the chapters in the book is entitled "Writing It All Down."

- My Tottering Days *(Work in the Vineyard Is Almost Done):* In His plan for my life, He made provisions for me to use the wisdom I asked for as a child in the three jobs I had in my life. And best of all, I am using the story-writing skills that He allowed me to develop as a child to keep me busy in my retirement years and to help my fellowman with words that will comfort, even after I am gone.

MAKING THE CONNECTION

Some people say, "It always amazes me how fate offers us all the tools we need to do what we were always meant to do." No ma'am! Not "fate," but God! God gave me the wisdom to be good at writing stories, writing poetry, speaking publicly, encouraging others, etc., and these are things I have used throughout each aspect of my life.

Look back through your life for a bit, and see if you don't find that to be true for you as well. Mmm hmm, see? I told you. But don't let your perusing stop there. What is it that you have always loved to do and are good at? Since you have to work anyway, wouldn't it be wonderful if you had a job that allowed you to do what you love and are good at? And better yet, you could incorporate your love and zeal for the Lord into your work. I did just that as a teacher for thirty years, a housing coordinator for ten years, a minister's wife for forty-two years, and now as a writer.

So, while you are preparing for, dealing with, or just coming out of your storm, always look for the blessing in it while singing your Jesus song as you go along.

Blessing In and After the Storm

Just as a mother knows what to do and what to say
To her child who may be grown and far away,
My God knows how to brighten my day
To such a point that it fairly glistens
And how to give me a song that I will sing
To anyone who listens.

My **care package from the Lord** has arrived,
And I could not have been more surprised.
Even as I pen this blog post for you,
The tears of gratitude swim in my eyes

At the caring blessing that He sent.
Y'all, I cannot tell you how humble,
Cherished, and grateful I feel
That He watched everywhere my footsteps went,
Talking about Him in the valley and from the top of the hill.

I don't have adequate words to express
To you the way I feel I have been blessed.
You see, it means so much when you receive
A blessing whose magnitude shows God's touch.

I told Him that I would tell of His love
In every place and in every way that I know,
And that is what I have been trying to do.
Yet, when He sent that special blessing
With bells and whistles, just for me,
I was reduced to a sniffling and thankful bit of humanity
Who, as I have told you before, will sing
My song of His lovingkindness everywhere I go.

So, this last verse is to You, Lord.
I can't tell you how much I love You,
But I will continue to try to show
The glory that You have allowed in me
For the world to get to know.
For it is not by me that these words have been coined
But by You, masterful Father, You, Who are Number One!

Folks, I know that you know me well enough by now to know that I feel things deeply, whether bad or good. And I just want you to know that my heart is full this morning. I used to wonder how it would feel for my work to go viral…well, now I guess I know. My poem "Mark Your Storm in Green" has reached over 4,300 likes on Facebook, and a second one, "Nobody Wants to Hear about God," has reached

4,500 to date! And I can tell you again, "Look for your blessing in your storm, and prepare your heart and mind for your blessing when your storm is past."

§

Discussion Questions
1. How do storms change us?

_____

2. Does our suffering help someone else?

_____

3. Have you ever received a care package from the Lord? Have you shared that story with anyone?

_____

4. How does the Lord feel if we become angry with Him about trouble in our lives?

_____

For Further Reading
Deuteronomy 1:38, Joshua 1:6–9 KJV

LESSON 4

New Beginning (Job 42:10-12 NKJ)

§

AIM: To LEARN TO DEVELOP your own ministry (your forte in working for the Lord, the thing you like and do best).

Song: "God's Grace"

You say that the storm changed you by giving you a new attitude or renewed zeal for working for the Lord. You are going to take that new awareness of the God you serve, as mentioned in the latter chapters of the book of Job, and do dynamic work for Him, huh? Good! Now you can look upon the day you developed a new attitude toward the Lord as your birthday, the day you were reborn in your determined effort to do for the Lord. But don't get comfortable waiting for someone to tell you what work you can do for the Lord. I say that because you may tend to fall back into old, lackadaisical ways while waiting. If the storm has caused you to reevaluate your life to the point that you have dropped some of your old habits, or, as I said, if you have a burning desire to do something—anything—for God, give in to it. Find something you like to do that benefits others, and do it with all your might while giving God the glory. If you do that, then you will be developing your own ministry, as mentioned in our lesson aim. You must fill up that newly created void with something new, or the old will return.

This book is being published in the springtime, and while that is coincidental, it works well for my point right now. As the poem below says, spring is a time for new beginnings, a time for planting new crops. What better time to develop a new ministry for the Lord as you aerate the garden soil of the word through the life you live?

Spring

A time for new beginnings is what I always
Think about when I think of Spring.
This season gives me a joy different from
Any that the other seasons bring.
It brings to mind renewal, such as we
Have built into our Christianity.

There is in me a joy that wants to swell.
There is in me optimism that wants to be let loose.
There is in me joyful love that
The life-giving God put there.
So, emerge from your chrysalis, butterflies of
Joy, optimism, and love.
Take winged flight, and soar high above,
Spreading your wonderful selves o'er the skies
To cause to spring forth other butterflies
Of like such, to propagate the air with
Joy, optimism, and love.

How Do I Start My New Life?

* Start by reading Jeremiah 9:24 NKJ. In this verse, the Lord is telling us some things to do to give Him glory. I will paraphrase it for you. He tells us that if we have to boast about anything, boast about Him. He says to boast about His

lovingkindness, His justice, and His righteousness, because He delights in these things. Ladies, when I read that scripture, I was astounded. I had read my Bible through several times, but I had not seen that scripture! I thought to myself, "I can do that for God, and I don't have to wait to start." Here is a sample prayer that you can use if you would like to:

Prayer: Father, you have rekindled my hope, and I am going to keep working and serving You and doing what You would have me do. I praise You, I bless You, and I thank You as I brag on you, Father!

I was pleasantly surprised that He likes for us to brag on Him. That made me feel closer to Him and made Him seem more approachable to me. When I read that scripture, it made me see Him as a loving God. I know we have been told that He is loving, but that scripture reaches out to me and says that He wants to have a relationship with me. He is interested in what I say. He likes my prayers to Him. Hebrews 4:16 NKJ is a warm welcome mat to come to His throne and talk to Him. There are a lot of scriptures that exude warmth, but this one wraps me in its arms. Think about it: the great God of creation cares about me, about what I think, and wants me to feel comfortable before His throne. He is wonderful!

- Here is something else you can do as you continue to develop your ministry. If you know a sister or a brother who is always negative and never has anything positive to say about anything or anybody in the church, who is always running to you with this tidbit or that tidbit, nip that in the bud. How do you do this? Easy. The next time she comes running with her juicy tidbit, just tell her that if it is not positive, you don't want to hear it. You don't have to be mean-spirited when you say it, just firm. If you do that a couple of times, this brother or sister will stop running to you. Wouldn't it be nice if everyone acted like that? *Sigh.* It would make the church leaders' jobs easier, I can tell you that.

For example, if a situation that is too hot to handle has developed in a congregation, don't talk, talk, talk about it, because it will spread like gangrene or wildfire. If you have to talk about it, talk to the people involved and Jesus, and step on. If you are thinking about a situation in the past that you did not handle very well, ask the person(s) involved and Jesus for forgiveness, and move on. That was in your past before your attitude-changing storm, remember. What could you do to help to fix the situation? Ask the tattler what he or she would do if in that situation. Let's help her or him as much as possible by asking, "What would you do differently if this were your daughter, your mom, your brother, etc.?"

- Study and pray as you begin anew. We will talk more about these subjects in lessons 7 and 8, but you can start by identifying a favorite book of the Bible. You might start with your favorite childhood Bible story and expand by reading the surrounding chapters. Find a book that grabs you and is hard to put down; that is where you should start. Also, learn the books of the Bible. Become familiar with your "Judgment Day" book.
- Talk the talk and walk the walk. If all of us would walk and talk like we are living for Jesus, the Church would be number one again in growth among world religions. It happened once, and it can happen again. Be excited about the cessation of the storm that was in your life, and use that excitement to brag about the best Friend that you have ever found! Remember, enthusiasm and excitement catch. Make opportunities for the chance to talk with God. Look forward to your prayer sessions with Him. Become and stay excited to talk to Him. Talk to Him as though He is your best Friend;

confide in Him the way you do your dad. You will not be sorry; I can tell you that.

Case in Point—I cannot tell you how much prayer is needed when we face any new beginning. Here is a blog post of mine that will better explain the fervor I have about prayer and new beginnings:

Big Girl First Night

First night in apartment awakened
In the wee hours of the morn
By the sound of screaming and
The sound of a loud fire horn.

Fire began in our building, the apartment
Above and to the right of ours.
Evacuation done as a safety measure.
To hear that everyone was okay
Was indeed a pleasure.
Builder of meth lab, meth lab
Needs rehab.
Just sayin'.

Yesteryear, when the still blew up
No one was hurt except the owner
And the user of the still, for stills
Were made back in the woods.

Now they brew "stuff" in the heart of town
Where innocent babies, children,
And adults can be found.

"I will both lie down and sleep, For Thou alone, O Lord, dost make me to dwell in safety." (Psalm 4:8 NASB)

The poem describes an actual event that happened in our life on a Monday night. My daughter, who, is special, got moved into her first apartment with her roommate, and all seemed to be well. I did my usual mother's prayer for my daughter to be okay (1 Peter 3:12 NKJ), and I went on to sleep. I did have the usual uneasiness that any mother would have when the nest has been emptied of its last chick.

Well, the next morning, I received a phone call that shook me up. I was informed that there had been a fire in the building that houses my daughter's apartment, but that she and her roommate were both okay. I was informed that they had had to spend the night in a motel because the electricity had been disconnected due to the fire. I was so shaken up that I had to ask the caretaker to repeat what she had just said. She did, and I was okay with her answers. Of course, being the mother that I am, I wanted to talk to my baby and to lay my eyes on her, just to be sure she was okay and had suffered no lasting trauma.

In the meantime, we had to break the news to her dad. That, I knew, would be no mean feat, so I let the worker who called me do the honors. I knew that he would be wondering the same thing that I was: "*Why* did they *not call at 2:30 in the morning to tell us that our daughter's* apartment *building was* on fire?"

I made sure he was sitting down before I handed him the phone. You would have to know him to appreciate the wisdom of this decision. Yes, he had his usual yelling hysterics, etc. I interceded to say that our daughter *was okay. I had to say that two times before his eyes stopped rapidly blinking and looking buck-eyed. He held his chest like Fred Sanford used to do on Sanford and Son. I can have a good laugh about it now, but at the time I* just *wanted to see my child.*

But you know what? I did not know that when I asked the Lord to take care of and protect my daughter, He would show me just how well He could. When we talked to her on the phone and saw her thirty *minutes later, she told her little story and was as cool and unflappable as could be.*

What *I garnered from this fiery situation* was this thought: "*Jesus keeps His children." That means, in all times and in all situations, whatever the outcome, He is in control. That let me know that* my daughter's *caretakers were on the ball and were going to take care of my child. And get this—this is what is so sweet about His love: He let the caretaker be a lady who goes to the same church we do and who knows and likes my daughter very well. I see the hand of the Lord all through this. This situation tells me that if I am on a book tour in Timbuktu, He will take care of my daughter and me* both, *because He can be in all places at the same time. In other words, I don't have to worry, because whether I am there or not, He is the keeper; He is* ULTIMATE*!*

Woo! It's song-singing time, don't you know! The perfect song for this situation is *"He's Able."*

"Pray without ceasing," we are instructed in 1 Thessalonians 5:17 KJV. In short, I have been praying ever since my momma explained prayer to me when I was just eight years old. Prayer and I are no strangers to each other. I prayed/pray for:

* Every test I took as a child and all through my college years
* Each time I got into someone's car as a child and as a teenager
* Each day I entered my classroom to teach my students
* Each job that I had after retirement
* Each time my child left the house with friends
* Each time I sit to have a meal
* Each time I begin to write a new book
* Each time I begin a blogging session (quipsbyalma.blogspot. com)
* Each time I open my Bible to gain insight
* Each time trouble arises
* Each time something happens that causes me to marvel
* Each time I feel the need to talk with my Father so I can be enveloped in His love
* World peace and the safety of all children
* Mankind in general, but especially for people whose hearts belong to Him
* And so many other times (James 5:16 KJV)

By the way, each day is a new beginning.

Discussion Questions

1. What is new or additional ministry can you start? Can it be done alone?
2. What does the Bible say about singing to feel better?

3. What are some particular things a sister can do to develop her own ministry?

For Further Reading
Ephesians 4:22–24, 2 Corinthians 5 KJV

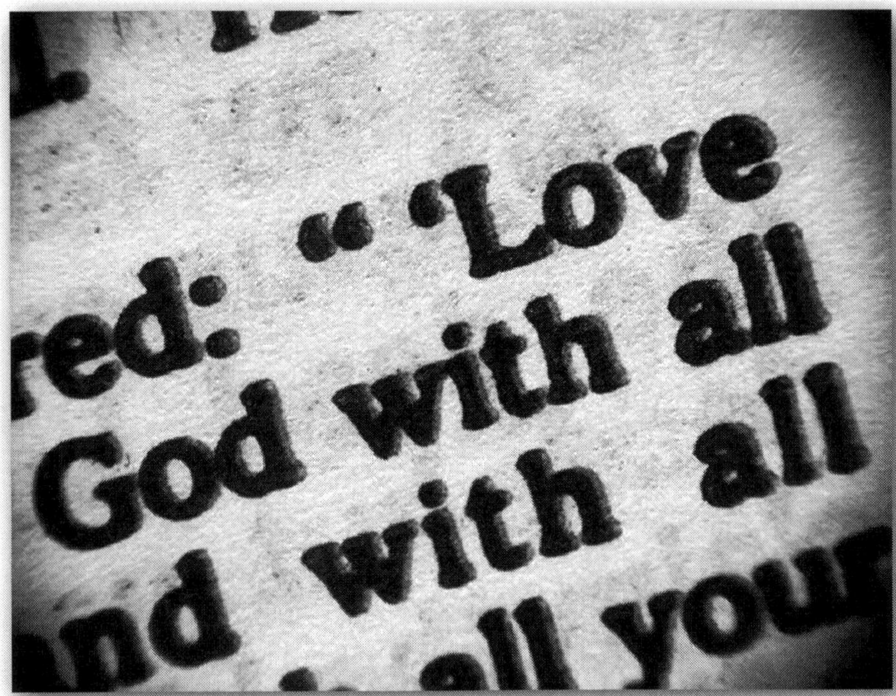

red: "'Love
God with all
nd with all
all your

Give It All You Have (Ecclesiastes 9:10 KJV)

§

AIM: To LEARN TO LEAVE no stone unturned in our quest to serve the Savior.

Song: "It's in My Heart to Serve the Lord"

Vessel of Clay

I commune with the Lord as a vessel
Of clay to its Father,
And I know that He listens and that
It really is no bother.

When I talk to Him, I tell Him about how
Much I love, adore, and thank Him
For loving me in spite of my faults
When my Christian light grows dim.

"From a vessel of clay to the
Omnipotent Artisan at the wheel,
Just another one of my rhymes
To tell you how I feel.

You are worthy to be praised,
Awesome, and all wise,
And I thank You for watching over
Me with Your all-seeing eyes."

I wrote this poem to remind me to say to others, "If you see/hear me doing/saying/writing something that you admire, do not attribute it to me. Attribute it to my Father, who according to Isaiah 50:4 MSG, allows His glory to shine forth through me."

She was determined and strengthened
In her resolve
To help out as best she could
And to work at getting problems solved.

I see so many people who will not do much to serve the Lord because they feel that they cannot do as good a job as Sister So-and-So. What we need to remember, ladies, is that the Lord didn't say that you have to be perfect to serve Him. He just said, "Go." He didn't say that you have to be the best speaker; just do what you do. Remember the old saying, "The forest would be mighty quiet if nothing but the best songbirds sang." Use your gift, whatever it is, for His glory. And another thing about the Sister So-and-So thing: if He had wanted you to be like Sister So-and-So, He would have made you her twin.

Remember, not everybody is a Mary, a Hannah, or an Elizabeth. You do what you can do!

"I Am Thine, Oh Lord"

Sometimes I feel the need to say, "I am Thine, oh Lord," though I know He knows this already. I just have to tell Him, "Use me how You will." I get so filled up that I feel like Jeremiah: "Fire shut up in my bones" (Jeremiah 20:9 KJV). So, I write, speak, sing a little, listen, counsel, pray with and for my fellowman, etc., all to be a source of encouragement as I allow myself to be used for God's glory.

That means that we all can put zeal in whatever we do in our daily life, in our duties, job, etc. How about it? Wouldn't it be nice if we put as much zeal into our work for the Lord as we do into hollering at ballgames? The church would be on fire once again, wouldn't it? Sure it would, because excitement is contagious. Make an imprint on somebody's life with your enthusiasm for the Lord.

* We are talking about developing your forte for the Lord. One of the simplest things we can do is love and give a smile. If you see a sister wearing a pretty dress or hear one singing well in worship or hear one speaking well at a ladies' day, or if you hear of a person doing an extremely kind deed, compliment that person. It cost you little and gains you and the church a lot. It will help to cultivate the feeling of loving and closeness you see in some congregations. Make sure your friendly smile is one that members see regularly and that visitors see should they visit the congregation where you attend worship.

Prayer: Dear Lord, make us ladies whose hearts are on fire for You as we try to be the kind of women that the church needs.

Case in Point—I remember back many years ago, I was in the third grade, and my mother finished explaining to me about prayer and Jesus. I take up the narrative after her initial explanation to me. I never will forget my response to her. I said, "You mean I can get a doll like Rita got?" *(You can read the beginning of this narrative in lesson 8 under the Case in Point section.)* You can see from the response above that our little third grader jumped on what her momma said just as she did most things. Her mother took the time to explain to her that she should never ask Jesus for trivial things like a doll. She explained what a special privilege it was to be allowed to pray to Him.

Needless to say, that little third grader took a lesson from this conversation that changed my life for the better. The lasting thing I took away from that conversation with my momma was that if you pray to Jesus, He will hear your prayer and answer it in His own good time. I coupled that teaching with other things I had heard my momma say and things I had heard my Sunday-school teacher say. I surmised that if I worked hard and tried to be a good girl, then Jesus might hear me sooner. I was taught to pray and learned to wait in patience for the Lord to answer my prayer(s). That premise has carried me over many a mountain and through many stormy patches in my life as I continue chopping my row. Learning to wait made my faith in Jesus stronger.

Somebody once said, "If you do what you have always done, you will get what you have always gotten." That is so true, but in this case, it applies in a positive sense. Since I have always prayed and have gotten answers aplenty, I continue to pray. Somebody else said, "If it ain't broken don't fix it." In other words, my prayer connection was not broken, so there was no need to fix it. I kept it going as I always had. I gave my work to the Lord my very best, and I did not allow anyone to deter me for long. When I fell, I got back up, prayed for forgiveness, and kept giving my best to the Lord. I thought about all those men and women in biblical days who had remained faithful, even in dark times, and were blessed for it. That simple childhood logic has stood me in good stead, and I thank the Lord for the momma He gave me and for the Sunday-school teachers He placed in my path.

And, folks, that is why you will hear me say that my motto is "Doing What I Can, While I Can." I give it all I have, and I keep stepping.

Case in Point 2 "How Do You Know?"—If you haven't taken the opportunity to read my book *W.O.W. created w.o.w.*, you really should do just that. Borrow a copy from somebody or request your library to get it if they don't already have it. It will bless you. Read the short story about Alicia on pages 34–39. You will be glad you did!

Just as Alicia did in *W.O.W. created w.o.w.*, I had been praying and waiting for something all my life, but I didn't know when I received it. That is why this Case in Point is entitled "How Do You Know?" Some of you are probably sitting there thinking, "How can you ask for something and not know when you have received it? That is just plain illogical!" To that thought I say, hold on there, my friend. Not so fast. That very thing can happen.

Let me explain it to you a little better than I have. I had been praying since I was a child for this thing. You know what I had been praying for all that time? I had been praying for Jesus to let me *be somebody one day.*

That is simple enough, I know. But, at what point do you know that you are somebody? You see, the audience that made me feel insecure in the first place is no longer the audience I am playing to now, is it? Nope, it's not. When I became a teacher, I was around other teachers, and I was no better or no worse than the others. I was nothing special. I was just a teacher who cared. Now, don't get me wrong; I thanked the Lord for allowing me to become a teacher, but I still was not at the top of my game yet. I didn't think so, anyway. When I was included in the Who's Who Among America's Teachers, I still didn't understand. I was just one of many. I was too busy making sure I did all I could to help my kids and to be caring at the same time. When I did think about the prayer prayed in earnest all those years ago, I thought, not yet. I have not arrived yet—nope, not yet. I am still one among many.

When my husband became a preacher, and the sisters in the church wanted to dress as I did, I thought, No biggie. It's just because he is in the limelight. It has nothing to do with me. When I was expected to speak at ladies' days, that was no big deal either. Many preachers' wives do that. I was one among many.

When I wrote my books, it was not until my third one that someone said something that bothered me a little. Let me tell you, briefly, what happened. I ran into a young lady I had taught who had not seen me in a while. She threw her arms around me and squealed and said she was so glad to see me. Then she told me she wanted to get all three of my books. I told her they were on Amazon, and she could get them there. She became a little hostile and said that she wanted to get her books right then, because she wanted me to sign them. I told her I didn't have any books with me. She became more hostile and yelled out, "Why not?" I tried to shush her and told her that I did not have the money to order any more right then, as I had just finished a book signing. I still didn't get the picture of what was bothering her until reflecting upon the conversation, later. I realized then that some people were so bent on telling me not to change, when they, themselves, were acting funny over the publishing of a book. It seems that once you become a published author or get any other measure of what some folk perceive as success, people will accuse you of having gotten the "big head" because of your perceived success. That is just the nature of some people. Nevertheless, I did my best to assure her that I am the same as I have always been. I made sure that would not happen again. I keep books with me always now.

Now here is the finale of this little case in point.

In case you have not read the book *Tallest Mountain in My World*, let me give you a little background info. A pan of cornbread mysteriously appeared at our house one school day evening, and my momma made me say that I had cooked it. I hadn't, but that didn't matter. These are the type of matches that we had to use to light the gas stove to cook the cornbread.

She made me cook cornbread every day from then on. I hated those old "book" matches and still do to this day because I was not quick enough with the movement of my fingers to keep from feeling the heat of the flaring match.

At any rate, I was to remember the matches and the cornbread years later.

As a preacher's wife, you are supposed to be able to cook. Okay, no biggie, right? Here is what happened to me not very long ago. I periodically take meals to various church functions. I was checking to see what was needed so I could help another church with their food preparation. I was told what to bring, and I said, "Okay." Then I was told, "Bring some of that cornbread of yours, but leave it in the car." It was to be taken to a particular house. Another time I was told to fix some dishes but to be sure and make some cornbread as well.

Those words about the cornbread astounded me to the point that I said aloud, but to myself, "Cornbread? It's just cornbread!" Those words took me back to when I was eight years old and I had to fix my first pan of cornbread. Then it hit me. The Lord had looked down the road in my life and made sure that I could cook a fine pan of cornbread. Then I thought about the other things that had happened in my life. I thought about the week before, when a former student of mine called me a "phenomenal woman"; about the great number of responses when I posted something on Facebook; about the number of birthday well wishes I received; about people's reaction to me when they hear I am an author, etc. That is when it hit me, folks: "Alma Jones, the Lord has answered your prayers and allowed you to become somebody!"

Wow! I was bowled over when I realized what the Lord had done in my life. Now, y'all know how introspective I can be, so I went back through my life, and I thought about the things I could do well now. As a little girl, I used to play at being a teacher. I used to write stories for my friends. Even back then, folks, He was preparing me for what lay ahead. And as far as being a preacher's wife, He prepared me by making sure that I was close to Him. Wow! What a wonderful, mighty God we serve!

What do I do with this newfound knowledge? I make sure that I do my best to give Him glory through my daily living. Humbly, I say, "Thank You, Lord!"

You have been through a storm, and you are determined to give your best to the Lord, and that is admirable; however, never forget that it is not over until it is over. It won't be over until the end of time. What this means is that we must keep going, no matter what, if any, other stormy sessions we have due to the adversary, and no matter the pain.

In this life, things will get rough from time to time because of the adversary. Just keep remembering that all is never lost, though the price of continued faith is often exorbitant. You must remember to keep those rose-tinted glasses on. Be mindful of the fact that if you give up on your faith, the next step is that you will give up on GOD. Then the adversary has you just where he wants you, at his mercy—and he has none! Just you keep your hands in the faithful hands of the Lord, keep giving it your best, and He will make everything all right. Keep going; don't stop. Keep blooming and sending up that sweet-smelling savor for the Lord. He will handle all else. Just like Job in the Bible, we have to keep going. How long did Job continue to be faithful to the Lord? He was faithful until his change came. He waited on the Lord. We have to do the same. Continue to be steadfast or begin to be steadfast. Give it all you have!

(Deuteronomy 6:5 KJV).

Will and Grace

Do the best you can as you chop your row,
But you cannot count on thanks from others you know,
Some will plant cockleburs, Johnson grass, and other
Weeds on your row, thus making it hard to hoe.

But one thing I have learned in my days
Of chopping, hoeing, and tilling in this garden below
Is that it is by His will and His grace that I thrive
In this garden, in spite of the sowing of weeds by the foe,
And I do not waiver in my resolve or in my zeal
To that eternal, blessed, and placid place to go.

§

Not the Greatest but My Best

Not the greatest poet to ever live
But what the Lord has blessed me
With, I freely give.

He blessed me with the heart
To reach the mind of the young,
To remind you that He sees
And cares about everyone, and
Yes, for you, young person too,
About every word that might
Flippantly roll off your tongue.

Ladies, use the gifts and talents that He
Has blessed you with, to help some
Of the less fortunate to deal with
Their burdens that are, at times, cumbersome.

You say you have no special talents
Like some of your other friends.
That is not true; you have to search and ask
For it, and it will be revealed to you.

What is it that you are good at
And that you like to do?
I hope that you ponder doing
A new or additional work as
You are reading and thinking about
This book that I have written for you.
*(I have shared this poem with you to show you how embracing something
that you love with zeal can grow your ministry, To God be the glory!)*

You know, it has been nearly six years since I published my first poem on my blog! So many yesterdays ago. I went back to my very first post on my blog, and guess what? I was a bastion of optimism then and still am today.

Surety

I have a surety within me that
Everything is going to be all right,
That I'm reaching the end of these trials,
That I'm nearing the end of my night.

There is a sturdy growth of hope, happiness,
And joy that is budding from seeds within my soul.
There is a metamorphic rock of renewed faith
Being unearthed for all who will to behold.

As the dawn breaks, because
Night time is o'er,
My soul rejoices because
My troubles will be no more.

Six Years Later—Answer to Surety

Have learned to speak to souls, myself included
Words of encouragement and of comfort
By using the gift that has been granted me.
I never thought that being a poet would
Be my retirement destiny,

Yet I love doing it, because writing words
Of inspiration is a gift that sets men free.
And I am so glad that this is one of the gifts
That was given in a blessing to me.

Discussion Questions

1. Read Ecclesiastes 9:10 KJV. What should the title of lesson 5 mean to a Christian?

2. Explain Isaiah 50:4 MSG.

3. What scripture from today's lesson could be interpreted as "Use me how You will, Lord?"

4. Why is it important to greet visitors with a smile?

For Further Reading

Colossians 3:23–24, Colossians 3:17, 1 Corinthians 16:14, 2 Corinthians 3:5 KJV

I praise You in all I do, Lord, because You have brought me this far.

LESSON 6

Close to Jesus (Ephesians 1:5-6 KJV)

§

Aim: To LEARN HOW TO be close to Jesus and to learn about the benefits of such a relationship.

Song: "Jesus"

He Loves Me

He loves me and I know it
And that is why I tell the world
"I love Him" and proudly show it!

§

It Will Show

You cannot keep company with the Lord
And not have it rub off on you.
Just as it showed on the apostles,
It will show on us too!

INTRODUCTION

You know, if I were doing this lesson for a ladies' day, the first thing I would do is to ask all the young ladies to stand. After they had all stood, I would thank them for attending and then have them take their seats. You see, I would have their attention right then. I would tell them that even if their momma, grandma, aunt, lady down the street, etc. had dragged them here today, they were here because the Lord wanted them here. I would tell them, "Yeah, I know that you had other things to do on a Saturday morning—if nothing else but sleeping in. But there is something that He wanted you to get from today's lesson. So, listen up, young ladies. Pick up what He wants you to get. For remember, He is ever mindful of us and is always carrying out plans for our lives. One more thing I want to ask you, young folks. Do you pray? Do you think that the Lord hears you when you pray? This poem is to give you something to think about."

When Children Pray

I found out a long time ago that
When children pray, Jesus listens,
Because children have not become calloused
By the world nor jaded by sin.
(We are a part of God's family
Young folks, He's waiting and listening)

Now, to move on to the rest of the lesson, when we are close to Jesus, we are teaching someone else to be close to Him, too. Don't you know that is the way of the world? That is what we are to do as we chop our row in the Lord's garden. We cultivate and help grow productive souls in others through the things they see us do. The world seems to say, "If it is good to you, then sister I want some, too!"

Case in Point—If your friend told you about a great sale on dresses, housewares, rings, etc., most of us would break our necks getting down to the sale to see what we could find for ourselves. We would say to ourselves, "What? She got hers, and I want mine! Maybe I can find something for myself." Ladies, y'all know how we do…

Well, it works the same way with the Lord. If you keep talking about His goodness, smiling through your trials, etc., the world will want to have a close relationship with Him, too. Why? Because they see the good contentment that the relationship has brought to you, and they want some of it. It is as simple as that. Remember that He said, "If I be lifted up, I will draw all men unto me" (John 12:32 KJV).

OTHER BENEFITS OF BEING CLOSE TO HIM
*I can because **I Am** delighteths in me, and I will skip and tell of His goodness wherever I go.*

If you are close to the Lord, you walk with an assurance that other church members and the world will notice. When you are close to Him, you handle your rough times a little differently than most folks. Because of all the times in your life that He has been there for you, you know that you are never alone, even when you cannot seem to find Him. You have learned from what the preacher has said and what other Christians have said and from your own track record

with Him that He is able and that He has a purpose for everything that happens in your life. You also know that nothing can happen to you without His knowledge. So you walk on with assurance. The world sees this assurance, and your brothers and sisters in Christ see it, too. Let me tell you a little story from my life. Look at the picture that follows, and I will begin my story.

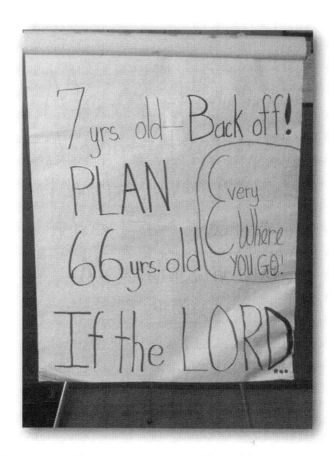

As the picture says, I was seven years old, and being a typical seven-year-old from back in the day, I had my share of curiosity. My mother had gone to work, and as was my custom, I was at my aunt's house, waiting for my favorite cousin to finish her lunch so we could go outside and play. I took out a big safety pin from my pocket and was closing and unclosing the head of the pin. Then I took note of the shiny new electrical socket that was at the end of a shiny new pipe in the kitchen. The socket was at eye level for me, a seven-year-old.

At school, we had been studying about circuits and dry cell batteries and doing experiments with electricity. My teacher said that copper was a good conductor. I remembered a class experiment with a dry cell battery and how a piece of copper had turned on a bulb on the other end, because it made a circuit. So, curious me wondered if the safety pin in my pocket could be a conductor. I knew that electricity was not supposed to go through big ol' me, so I thought, "Well, wonder what it will do?" Yes, ladies, I can hear you gasping in your minds and thinking, "Don't tell me that you stuck that pin in that socket." Yep, you guessed it! That's what I did. I stuck that pin in that socket.

Now, you know that a 110 circuit will hold on to you. I have found out that these days they make them so they actually throw you across the room. I don't know about that, but I do know that that socket did not throw me anywhere. *(The moment of contact is still fuzzy in my mind. I did carry the brown imprint of the pin on my middle finger and thumb of my right hand for several months and I am cautious about plugging things into electrical sockets to this day.)* The lights went out immediately. My cousins all screamed, and my aunt came running into the kitchen with her ironing cord. She held a candle and a book of matches. They lit the candle, and she asked what had happened. All my cousins started crying and avowing that they did not know. She held the candle up to the only outlet in the room and roared, while all of my cousins gave a collective gasp. She said, "Who put that pin in that socket?" Nobody said anything, and she said she was going to line them all up and start beating until somebody told her who put that pin in that socket.

I thought to myself, "If I can just get by her, I'll be out this door like greased lightning, and I'm going home!" I was not going to tell on myself, and neither was anybody else, because it had been my pin and nobody knew I had it—or so I thought. The cousin who was first in line to receive a whipping with the ironing cord yelled out, without preamble, "I know who had that pin! Louise (meaning me, as that was the childhood name that I went by) did, because I saw her with it." I could not believe it; my favorite cousin told on me!

My aunt trained her angry eyes on me and yelled, "Did you stick that pin in my socket?" I was so terrified, I couldn't answer. I don't remember what else she said right then, something about whipping me, to which I remember replying, "Please don't tell my momma on me. She might be mad at me." My aunt said that she was going to whip me herself. I remember replying something like, "Momma said nobody better not whip me, 'cause I am the only girl she has." Then I started crying in earnest and said again, "Auntie, please don't tell Momma on me." I was hoping that she would listen, and she did!

She said, "I am going to tell your momma, and she is gonna beat your backbone!" As I was sidling by her, she asked me if I had felt anything run up my arm. I said, "No, ma'am," to which she told me again what my momma was going to do to me when she got home.

Now, I told you all that to make a point...but look at this next picture first.

When Moses (Exodus 1:9, 15, 22; Exodus 2:15 KJV), Joseph (Genesis 37:18 KJV), Daniel, (Daniel 6:16 KJV), and the Hebrew boys (Daniel 3:15–20 KJV) were in danger of death, God saved them because He had a plan for them. So I don't know why He told that electric current, "Back off!" and sent it running the opposite way back down through the apartment building so that it burned out fuses and wires in several other apartments…and I don't know why I only received an imprint of the pin burned into my left hand, but I do know that *if God is for you, nothing can be against you* if He has a plan for you. And yes, to answer your unspoken question, I do wonder sometimes what He saved me for. I know why He saved Moses and the rest of them, but I just don't know what He saved me for. Then I think to myself, "Well one thing about it, if God is for you, who can be against you?" (Romans 8:31 KJV).

Look at the next picture.

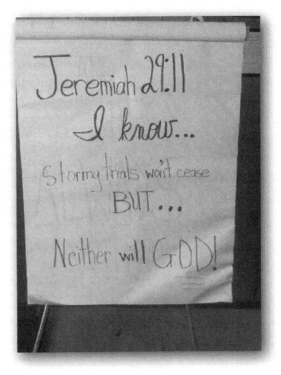

No matter *who* or *what* comes up against you in your life, if you are close to Him, I can tell you to trust Him and lean on Him, even through your tears, and remember He has a plan for your life (Jeremiah 29:11 KJV). Look at the next picture.

(Psalm 16:1 NASB)
(Revelation 15:2 NASB)

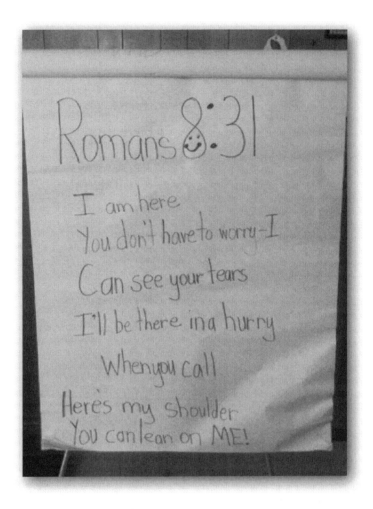

The last two pictures shown above, and the words to this favorite song of mine (Kirk Franklin, "Lean on Me") say it all! We know that God is going to win, because the Bible has already told us that. So, though I do not know why He saved me, I do know that you cannot find a better general than God Almighty, the Great **I Am**! As it says in Romans 8:31 (KJV), "If God is for us, then who or what can be against us?"

Prayer of Thanksgiving to My Father

When I faced the Johnson grasses, cockleburs, and morning glories of life, you did not leave me alone. You kept by my side as You taught me how to chop my row and how to wield a sharpened hoe, and for that and all of Your care, I thank You!

How to Get Close to Him

You might be thinking, "Yes, Sister Jones, but how do I get close to Him?" Good question. Here is what you must do to develop an intimate relationship with Him.

- Develop your faith. If you already have faith in Him, then deepen it. Here is how you do that. Romans 10:17 KJV says that "Faith cometh by hearing and hearing by the word of God."
  1. In short, come to worship so that you can hear the word being preached.
  2. Come to Bible classes and Sunday school so that you can listen to and participate in discussions.
  3. Lastly, before you begin each study session, read your Bible and ask the Lord to open your understanding. We are a people who walk by faith and not by sight (2 Corinthians 5:7 KJV).
- You can never have too much faith. Mark 9:24 KJV tells us to pray for a stronger faith if our faith is weak.
- Another thing to do to keep or get close to God is to love your brothers and sisters. In John 13:34–35 KJV, the Bible tells us to "Love one another." It further says that "By the love that we have for one another, men will know that we are His." That means that we have to love at all times, and not

just when folk are behaving themselves. Walk the walk and talk the talk: show your love for the Lord by showing love to your fellowman.

For Each Day

I am thankful for each day that the Lord allows me to live,
For it is another day that I can share the love that to me
He so freely did give.

No Greater Love

You loved me enough that
For me Your blood You shed.
You loved me enough that
You created me.
You love me enough that
You sustain me.
You loved me enough that
You give me a purpose by
Endowing me with a gift(s)
And allowing me to serve
So that I feel useful and contented.
You love me enough that
To green pastures I am led.
You love me enough that
By your loving hand, I am fed.
"You are Mine and I will come again
And gather you unto Myself, for
I AM faithful" is what You said.

Kept by the greatest love of all—
My Father, My God, My Savior!

Life taught me, close to Jesus always to stay and to
Be thankful for the love that has come our way
And give some of it away today.
Who did you entertain unawares yesterday?

DISCUSSION QUESTIONS
1. Explain Ephesians 1:5–6 KJV.

_____

_____

2. What does John 12:32 KJV mean to us as Christians today?

_____

_____

_____

3. What are the benefits of a close relationship to the Lord?

_____

_____

FOR FURTHER READING
Titus 2:13–14, John 1:16, Psalm 46 KJV

Gleaning from the Word (1 Peter 2:2 KJV, Hebrews 11:6, 2 Timothy 2:15 KJV)

§

AIM: To LEARN HOW TO study to be blessed by prayerfully studying the Bible..

Song: "Holy Spirit"

> *My Father provided the Bible for me to study, and it enhanced my faith so that I could walk past my pain and find joy again.*

§

My Chapter

Like the Easter egg hunt when we were kids,
The simple is made joyful beyond measure
By the searching for and finding of the treasure.

For I found my chapter
That You had written so long ago.
You knew one day that such as I
Would wonder where You were
When I uttered my cry.

While reading my Bible one day,
I came upon a passage that I can claim as mine,
But never in my wildest dreams did I think
An entire chapter I would find.

This chapter I am referring to is Psalm 71 KJV. This passage of
scripture has a special significance to me, and we will discuss it in
a bit. I will show you how this chapter blessed me during a stormy
time in my life. It will be a good thing to have in your arsenal of faith
against the day when you are hit by your storms. But before we begin
to discuss it, I want to make a couple of points about the need for and
the benefits of studying.

"Desire the sincere milk of the word that you might grow thereby"
(1 Peter 2:2 KJV) You see, your faith may be strong now, because
you just finished getting out of your storm and you are running
on the excitement of His deliverance. But what the Lord knew
when He had the Bible penned was that when that enthusiasm
began to dampen—because of time, other onslaughts, etc.—our
faith would tend to wane. Folks, we walk by faith and not by sight
(2 Corinthians 5:7 KJV), and you can never have too much faith.
The Bible says that without faith, it is impossible to please Him
(Hebrews 11:6 KJV). "Faith is the victory that overcomes the
world" (1 John 5:4 KJV). If you keep your faith when the ordinary
person loses it, that says something about you to God. Just as He
rewarded Abraham and all of those people of faith who are written
about in Hebrews 11 KJV, He will reward you and me, too. But we
gotta keep the faith!

* We need to study to learn and remember what a powerful
God we serve. As I said in the paragraph above, you may
tend to forget what He has brought you through after you
get comfortable and your storm is far behind you. In other

words, the row that we are chopping may not have any weeds, morning glories, cockleburs, or patches of Johnson grass for a while, so we become complacent.

- It is a proven scientific fact that if we eat less, our stomachs will shrink. The same thing will happen to our spiritual bodies; if we do not feed the inner man, he will shrink. Regular, *prayerful* study of the Bible will cause your faith to grow (1 Peter 2:2 KJV).

- Another thing, did you know that if you study your Bible often enough, certain passages of scripture will stay with you longer than others? You will find yourself going back over and over again to certain ones because they soothe your soul so much, and before you know it, you will have memorized them. Let me tell you, there is something about memorizing scriptures that will change your attitudes and outlook and strengthen your prayer life. You will get to a point where you look forward to your meditation time because you will be wondering what the Lord is going to show you next. Why does it work that way? It is the way God set it up. Remember that He said, "Desire the sincere milk." (1 Peter 2:2 KJV) Your knowledge of the scriptures will become a noticeable part of you that others will copy. Yep, you will have become a trendsetter. And how do you think God looks at you when He sees you working to memorize scriptures? Yes, it pleases Him!

- Study, because the Bible was written to teach mankind about the welfare of the soul (Romans 15:4 KJV). These same words will judge us in the last days (John 12:48; Revelation 12:20 KJV).

All right now, back to how Psalm 71 KJV blessed me in a stormy time in my life. I have highlighted parts of this psalm to make it easy for you to make a connection with the scripture and see one instance of how prayerfully studying my Bible helped me. I think that this breakdown of the chapter will bless you.

Psalm 71 New King James Version
1 In You, O LORD, I put my trust;
Let me never be put to shame.
2 Deliver me in Your righteousness, and cause me to escape;
Incline Your ear to me, and save me.
3 Be my strong refuge,
To which I may resort continually;
You have given the commandment to save me,
For You *are* my rock and my fortress.
4 Deliver me, O my God, out of the hand of the wicked,
Out of the hand of the unrighteous and cruel man.
5 For You are my hope, O Lord GOD;
You are my trust from my youth.
6 By You I have been upheld from birth;
You are He who took me out of my mother's womb.
My praise *shall be* continually of You.
7 I have become as a wonder to many,
But You *are* my strong refuge.
8 Let my mouth be filled *with* Your praise
And with Your glory all the day.
9 Do not cast me off in the time of old age;
Do not forsake me when my strength fails.
10 For my enemies speak against me;
And those who lie in wait for my life take counsel together,
11 Saying, "God has forsaken him;
Pursue and take him, for *there is* none to deliver *him.*"
12 O God, do not be far from me;
O my God, make haste to help me!
13 Let them be confounded *and* consumed
Who are adversaries of my life;

Let them be covered *with* reproach and dishonor
Who seek my hurt.
14 But I will hope continually
And will praise You yet more and more.
15 My mouth shall tell of Your righteousness
And Your salvation all the day,
For I do not know *their* limits.
16 I will go in the strength of the Lord GOD;
I will make mention of Your righteousness, of Yours only.
17 O God, You have taught me from my youth;
And to this *day* I declare Your wondrous works.
18 Now also when *I am* old and gray-headed,
O God, do not forsake me,
Until I declare Your strength to *this* generation,
Your power to everyone *who* is to come.
19 Also, Your righteousness, O God, *is* very high,
You who have done great things;
O God, who *is* like You?
20 You, who have shown me great and severe troubles,
Shall revive me again
And bring me up again from the depths of the earth.
21 You shall increase my greatness,
And comfort me on every side.
22 Also with the lute, I will praise You—
And Your faithfulness, O my God!
To You, I will sing with the harp,
O Holy One of Israel.
23 My lips shall greatly rejoice when I sing to You,
And my soul, which You have redeemed.
24 My tongue also shall talk of Your righteousness all the day long;
For they are confounded,
For they are brought to shame
Who seek my hurt.

You might be wondering what pointed me to Psalm 71 KJV. Well, every morning I read a devotional magazine called *Power for Today*, and my reading for a particular day sent me to Psalm 71 KJV. As is my habit, I dutifully went there to read. What I read there stroked my soul and made my doubts and fears take a backseat indeed!

Now, I have been dealing with enemies and/or life problems for a good long while, but I just pray, ask for help, and keep on stepping. Do you remember when I told you that you can deal with a "storm so long that it becomes your norm"? That is what happened to me. But, if you recall, I told you that when your enemies see that you are weathering your storms well, then they will increase their torturing and troubling ways. I'm sure some of you reading this know something of what I am talking about.

Well, let me tell you—my enemies upped the pressure so much this week that it knocked me to my knees! I found myself trying to pray right in the midst of the new onslaught, but I got no relief. Nevertheless, I didn't stop pushing forward. I found myself asking the Lord if He could hear me and if He cared about me still. Let me continue to break this on down to you so you will see why I say this chapter is mine. I reminded the Lord that I had been depending on Him since I was a child and asked this: since He had allowed me to develop an intimate relationship with Him in which I could lean on Him, why was He deserting me now? I asked Him if it was because of my age.

Let me tell you, folks, I had a good old pity party when I talked with the Lord. Some of y'all know the drill; you know how we do when the bottom falls out and it seems like it is going to stay out. We cry and pray and pray and cry, and sometimes we resort to whining as we talk to Him. Yes, folks, no need for me to plead the Fifth; I confess I did all of the above. I reminded Him that I had not only devoted my life to Him but had also written a volume of praise of His marvelous wonders. I told Him about how people looked up to me as a person of faith. Yep, folks, I pled my case just as Job did in the Bible. Then I told Him that I was nowhere around when He created the earth and laid its foundations. I told Him that I was just a mortal woman who was trying to find an audience with her Lord, Who could do all! Then I asked Him to stop my enemies by making them be at peace with me and to give me peace in my current situation while increasing my faith daily.

I finished my prayer, read my Bible, and called it a night. I followed this routine for three days. The difference was that on that third night, I determined, like Job, "Though He slay me, I'm yet going to trust Him." But oh, on the fourth day, I awoke with a feeling everything was going to be okay, until I rubbed the sleep out of my eyes and remembered my situation. Yet, I still had that strong resolve to keep on trusting Him, even if… By the fifth day, when I awoke, I knew in my heart and in my spirit that my situation was on its way to being rectified—and it was.

Now I said all of that to show you something important. Psalm 71 KJV, as it blessed me that morning, can be broken down like this:

Praying (verses 1 and 3)
Asking if He could hear (verses 2 and 12)
Asking if He cared like He used to (verses 9 and18)
Enemies (verses 4, 10, 11, 13 and 24)
Youth (verses 5, 6, and 17)
Used to Praising Him (verses 6, 8, 14, 15, 16, 19, 22, 23, and 24)
Known as a Person of Faith (verse 7)

Do you see the beauty in this chapter? Because the Lord looked down through time and saw my situation, He placed an encouraging section in the Bible to walk me through every emotion that I had this week! That is the kind of God we serve, and that is why I say, "I won't stop; I can't stop; I can't come down!" And another thing: if I had not had this awful time this week, some of you out there would still be floundering, but because my relief was so great when He blessed me, I then told you, and you were blessed too! And you want me to think that it was just coincidence that David recorded every one of my emotions in Psalms at the will of the God of all creation for me to read at this moment and on this day? Nuh uh! No coincidence, just blessings! Another care package!

Now, I always say that if the Lord has moved some mountains in your life and leveled some valleys, you ought to tell somebody. Do I still begin my day with prayer? Yes, I do. Do I still get bothered by things from time to time? Yes, I do, but you know what? I have learned to not linger on anything troublesome for long. I have, at long last, learned to lean on Him and trust Him in whichever direction He swings me. Do I think sometimes that I might fall? Yes, I do, but I know that as long as I keep my hand in His hand, He will lift me up again and set me on the right path under His protective wing. Then, folks, I step on. I step on through my pain, heartache, and all sorts of trouble, until He leads me to that gentle stream of still waters that is nestled in pastures of green (Psalm 23 KJV).

Remember: no matter what your problem is, keep praying, reading your Bible, and having faith in Him, for He will handle any and everything that troubles you, and He will refine you in the process so you can help someone else. I know, because I just did!

One Last Thought:

If you don't remember anything else I have said, remember this, "Paint your problems and life situations green for 'go,' and keep stepping on for the Lord." Here is an additional motto for my life: "Through it all, He will make a way somehow, because He takes care of His own."

(And to those of you who are impatient with my continued treatise on this subject matter, don't be. The day may come when you are in several troubles and will gobble this up and wish for more. We all are told to bear one another's burdens, and so we shall. Be blessed.)

§

At First

I read my Bible because I was told to at first,
But reading that Bible has created in me an unquenchable thirst
And a voracious appetite for feeding from God's word,
And I am learning deep things about which I have scarce heard.

§

I Know
I know
Thus, I grow.

§

Voracious Appetite

I was excited this year when Spring first arrived
Along with the usual signs of Spring:
The songbirds, the robins and baby birds
With tiny voices filling the air with
Their wee-throated chirping.
Oh, and lest I forget, there is that
Dreaded annual termite swarming.

That swarm is not something that
Any homeowner ever wants to see.

Well, guess what folks, the homeowner
Who saw them this time happened to be me.

Was I happy to see the winged insects whose voracious
Appetite could damage or bring my home down around me?
My answer to that needless query is a resounding, "No siree!"
Had to find capital for the depleted till
So that I could pay the exterminator's bill!
Did I allow this latest sign of Spring
To take my Spring found joy away from me?
No, not me, no siree,
Because when I looked out of my window
I found, with joy, that the hummingbird family,
Having made another pilgrimage back to me,
Was flying around for all to see.

Now, you know I would not be me if I
Did not make an application to the Lord by
Using this poem that I just wrote to prod
Us onward in our quest to please our God.
Would that we could be like the termite and the hummingbird
And feed with relentlessness upon the Written Word
And share the news with our fellowman, because it
Would be the best sharing that they had heard.

Yes, siree!

Look at the last verse of this poem. You can see that our sharing
the goodness of God is likened to being prepared through being
well-read in the Bible. This preparation allows us to be the vessel by
which our acquaintances can be fed.

DISCUSSION QUESTIONS

1. What does the Bible say about faith?

_____

_____

2. How does reading the Bible benefit us? How can our reading benefit our fellowman?

_____

3. According to 2 Timothy 2:15 KJV, why should we study?

_____

_____

FOR FURTHER READING

Romans 10:17, James 1:5 KJV

Young and old alike benefit from prayer!

How Important Is Prayer (Matthew 26:39, Hebrews 4:16 KJV)

§

AIM: To learn the "why" and "how" of prayer.

Song: "Pray on My Child"

Introduction

Ah, prayer—how important is it? Does it even work? Why bother? These are all questions that people have asked at various times in their lives. I do hope that when we finish this book, those of you who believe in prayer will be buoyed up further in that belief, and those of you who do not believe in it much, or perhaps not at all, will be willing to give it a try and be able to say:

Don't have the time or the inclination to worry about things I can't do anything about; therefore, said my prayers, moving on, and chopping my row so that His garden will grow.

Let's see, where shall I start? When I look back over my life and realize that the charcoal-bucket days are so many yesterdays ago, I marvel and am thankful, because I realize that it is by God's grace that I have come this far. I must say that I have waxed sentimental these last few days when looking back over my life and realizing that the Lord has blessed me to live to see my "one day." I think that I will start by giving you two poems and then a **Case in Point**, okay?

Gonna Be Somebody

Lived way below the poverty level,
Lived with just enough,
Lived with aplenty,
Lived with the Lord whether
The going was smooth or rough.

Lived below the poverty level
On cornbread, fatback, and dried beans.
Rice was a standard staple,
As were, when in season, collard greens.

Food was bought by the week,
And whatever was on sale
Made up the extra fare for the week.
Sometimes hominy, sometimes grits,
But always plenty to eat.

"Gonna be somebody," was my inner cry
And **kept praying to Jesus**
To allow it to come by.

No More Charcoal-Bucket Days

He brought me from the charcoal
Bucket and blackened walls
To a nice place in society, to install.
I won't complain about Him at all,

For He is my reason for living, y'all.
(excerpt from *Quipsbyalma.blogspot.com*)
James 5:16 NASB

§

Case in Point—I come from a poor, single-parent family; all my mother had to give me were her God, her morals, and her ideals, and I must say, that was enough. She always taught me to pray and "reach for the stars," and she told me time and time again that I was "bound to land among the treetops."

* I wanted to be a teacher or a nurse since I was nine years old. We had no money and could see no way for me to go to college, but I kept praying and believing—and "Voila!" I went!
* I wanted to be a writer, and "Voila!" I am!

I have not told you the entire path my life took, but I have told you enough so you can understand the determined mindset of the little girl in the following excerpt from my book *W.O.W. created w.o.w.*:

She hoped her cousins wouldn't give her a hard time about the water she was there to take. She knew that her aunt had started dropping hints about how high her water bill had been. She made it to her aunt's and knocked on the door.

"Who is it?" her favorite cousin called from within.

"It's me," Alicia piped up.

"Door's open; come on in."

Alicia went inside and started her routine of filling up the two canisters.

"Don't you ever get embarrassed about hauling that water? I wouldn't do it. That's what your brothers ought to be doing!" said her cousin.

"I know that's what my brothers ought to be doing," said Alicia. "But it's hard for Momma to make them do anything. You know they're teenagers, and she can't make them do what she wants them to do, and sometimes they make her cry. Somebody's gotta help Momma, so I do it. I don't want to see her cry. Sometimes I hear her crying at night, and I don't like to hear Momma cry. So, you know; I go get the water. It's okay. Now, about people laughing at me; they gotta laugh at something. If they didn't laugh at me, then they would be laughing at somebody else. Anyway, one day I'm gonna be somebody!"

§

She hoped she didn't meet any of her friends on the way home, because you could hear the water splashing against the sides of the canisters. By the time she got back home, Alicia's coat was wet on one side, because one of the canisters had developed a slow leak. She hung the coat up on the back of the door in the bedroom and closed the door. She hoped it would be dry tomorrow, because it was the only coat she had. It was so cold in the bedroom that maybe her coat would not dry, but she had to take the chance and leave it in the bedroom with the door closed, because she didn't want to smell like smoke when she went to school the next day.

Alicia couldn't worry about Hank Gould or anybody else right then. She had to cook. She knew it would do no good to worry about him.

She went back in the front room and put the rice on in the rice pot and rinsed the chicken with a cup of water. When the rice got done, Alicia set it on her makeshift table, the metal chair beside the charcoal bucket. Since there was no flour, she battered the chicken in meal and then put the frying pan on, with a small amount of lard to cook the chicken. Alicia remembered to use a very small amount of lard, because she knew the lard had to last for three or four weeks. Momma had taught Alicia how to stretch the lard. She knew to use the fatback grease for cooking cornbread. And she knew to put the fatback grease back in the grease can after she finished frying anything.

She browned the chicken on both sides and then poured the extra grease into the grease can. She then put one glass of water and one-fourth of an onion in the frying pan and let the chicken simmer. Alicia had to be careful that the water from the frying pan did not boil over onto the charcoal and put the fire out. She knew the room would be colder than it already was if the charcoal got wet. Then Alicia put more charcoal onto the charcoal bucket to warm the room a bit more.

Alicia got sick to her stomach because of the fumes from the charcoal as it started up. She had to go to the door to stick her head out and get fresh air so she wouldn't be sick. She always had a headache in the evenings because of the fumes from the charcoal bucket.

After she had finished cooking, Alicia again thought about her harrowing day at school. "But that's all right. That's okay;

one day, I'm going to be somebody, and I'm going to have pretty clothes, and ain't nobody gon' laugh at me then!"

Many of those high school days and nights, long after her mother had fallen asleep, Alicia would finally go to sleep herself, with her mother's words resounding in her brain and her prayers to Jesus on her lips: "Reach for the stars; I'm going to be somebody someday! Please help me to do it, Jesus; please help me." (excerpt from W.O.W. created w.o.w.)

* Back in one of the earlier lessons, we talked about having a track record. Well, when you have had some prayers answered, that should cause you to pray more.
* Prayer gives us the chance to have an audience with the potentate of potentates!
* Prayer allowed a little girl who used to have holes in her socks to be sent to the School of Polishing and Hard Knocks to come through blessed and grown and, at last, to come into her own (her "one day").

Prayer has shepherded me through all of my changes, both good and bad—the good so I could thank Him and remain humble, and the bad so I could remain faithful. To further illustrate my point, let me take you on a stroll back down memory lane for a bit.

Remember how you felt when that precious baby you brought home from the hospital said his first word, took his first step, got his first tooth, went to his first day of school, etc.? Those are all positive "firsts" aren't they? Sure they are!

But what about those other firsts—the day pain first invaded your baby's world and rocked you to your soul? The time when you ended up in the emergency room with a fiery-hot baby who, it turned out, had strep throat and an ear infection. The time when you had to pack that pride and joy of a baby boy in an ice bath because his fever was so high, and you couldn't get it to come down. The time when you walked the floor all night long because the baby was so sick he couldn't sleep, and neither could you. What about the time that you found out he was allergic to the antibiotic he was given, and he broke out in a rash that looked like chickenpox?

These are all times when you had to reach for your praying shoes.

Then the baby's fever broke, and you were able to put a tiny t-shirt on his fragile little body, and you gingerly placed him in his crib, which you had moved right next to your bed. But he was so fretful that you took your baby, lay him on your stomach, and he slept the rest of the night through. Remember the relief you felt when you knelt down in your mind's eye and you gave God some praise and thanks. You utilized prayer. Remember, too, that during that time you only dozed, because you stayed awake to keep feeling the baby's forehead and kiss his cheeks. You were so joyful that you kept thanking the Lord for making your baby well.

Now, I said all that to come to this point: just as we knew and still know how to take care of our babies, so does the Lord know how to take care of us. Why? We are HIS children, just like your baby is yours. The scriptures tell us that if we, being earthly, know how to give good gifts and take care of our children, how much more does our heavenly Father who cares for us and Who created us. We got our knowledge of how to take care of our children from Him. How much more does He know how to take care of us—and yet, we fail to ask. Sometimes we wring our hands and forget about the avenue of prayer. But what we need to do is talk to the Lord in the name of Jesus and tell Him all about our situations—and keep working as though He has already given us our answer. One thing I have found out about the Lord is that if you keep talking to Him and giving your problems over to Him, you will not worry about it anymore. I am telling you people, prayer has been and still is important in my life!

Added Benefits of Prayer

> No joy so great
> As that of an answered prayer,
> For it is a gentle reminder that
> I'm not forgotten by the
> Deity that dwells "Up There."

However, we don't always get the answer to our prayers as quickly as we want to. As I told you when we went through the lesson regarding the plan for our lives, lesson 1, everything happens for a reason, and the Lord does not have to tell us the reason for the various happenings in our lives. But it is nice when He lets us know He has not forgotten about us by doing what I call sending a care package. When you keep your faith by praying and persevering, it is so sweet when you get one of those tailor-made blessings that has your name written all over it—*a care package!* Tailor-made blessings come in all sizes, big and small. Often, the tailor-made blessings come while you are in the midst of a storm you have prayed about and are waiting desperately for an answer to. I am just so grateful for reminders great and small that the Lord is mindful of me. It makes me feel so special, as if I am one in a million! And if you have been starting your day with prayer and developing a closer relationship with Him, then you will feel the same way when you get one of those special blessings, if you don't already. Any way we say it, it is wonderful to be wrapped in the arms of His loving care, isn't it, ladies?

Remember that HE is still making plans for us, and that fact ought to keep us going when we get on the page where there are trials, tribulations, and trouble. What keeps me going is knowing that this page is not going to last always, because our Father, our Friend, still has plans for us.

BUILDING THAT PRAYERFUL RELATIONSHIP

* Our prayer life ought to be as regimented as breathing and eating and you know that nobody has to remind us to do either. We shouldn't get so busy with our jobs, duties, etc. that we don't plan for our spiritual meal. Let's not get so caught up in the affairs of this temporary home that we find ourselves saying things like "I meant to; I will; I just didn't have time; I'll make it up." Don't waste time trying to figure out an enemy that you could be using that as praying time.
* The Bible says in Romans 8:28 KJV, "All things work together for good for those that love the Lord." That means that God will work things out for us, no matter what our enemies plan, if we keep our faith intact and continue to pray. No matter what state we are in in our lives, we must never forget to pray. Have a set time to pray every day. Life will send you to His throne often, but you need to be well acquainted with Him. Read the poem below:

> Do you do your best talking to Jesus in the
> Wee hours of the morning before the break of day.
> Me too…don't know what it is about that time,
> But it is then that I can articulate best what I want to say.

> It is easy for me to approach His
> Throne at that early hour
> So that I can bask in His love and in
> His infinite sense of power.
> (excerpt from *DEI Sub Numine Viget*)

No matter what you are going through,
Begin your day with prayer, and peace of mind
Is what you will find.

Hebrew 4:16 KJV—Know this scripture, and put it into practice. I can never get enough of the knowledge and the experience of prayer, because *the more I learn the more I yearn.*

Are you a worrier or a prayer? I told you before that I have always been a deep thinker and that I spent thirty years as a teacher. Yes, if you guessed that I had my students thinking deeply, you are correct. I did indeed teach my students to become deep thinkers, for which, I still get thank-yous to this day. And you know, folks, all I was doing was performing my job by teaching my kids to *want* to learn by teaching them to *love* to learn! Maybe you did not hear me, so I am going to say it one more time. I taught my children to **want to learn by teaching them to love to learn**. And I have been trying to do the same thing for you. Say what? Yes, you heard me correctly. This isn't the case for all of you, because some of you are way ahead of me, and I applaud you. But for the sake of the others, stay with me as I break it down for them, okay?

You know what? How many of you have something on your mind that is worrying you? Sometimes as we are chopping our row for the Lord, the Johnson grass, morning-glory vines, and cockleburs get to be too much for us, and we feel that we cannot do it any longer. News flash! Worrying about it will not make it go away, but praying about it *sho* will. Yes, you heard me correctly. If you don't believe me, then listen to this brief case in point.

Case in Point—There was a time in my younger days when I had a big problem. I had worked it every way I knew how, and it was not getting any better. In fact, it seemed to be getting worse. One day I went to a gospel meeting, because it was my duty to go. The preacher was like a broken record, talking and talking and talking about the benefits of prayer. I was listening to the preacher, and I thought to myself, "You know, you are a really good speaker, but we both know life does not work that simply." I remember thinking, "I wish it were that simple." I never will forget, I looked at him and gave him a deadpan look while thinking, "Yeah, right!" In the end, he talked about prayer so much that I decided I would give it a try.

So, when I got home and got to a quiet place, I prayed about my problem. I knew it was not going to get any better, but I prayed again. Then went on to bed. Now, y'all know how we get when a problem is heavy in our hearts; we go to bed thinking about it and wake up thinking about that same problem. And that is exactly what I did. I woke up with the problem on my mind and...wait a minute! Something was different. I felt lighthearted. Then I started thinking about what had me so worried, and I realized the problem was still the same, but **I** was different! But how? I got to thinking that maybe it was because I prayed about that problem in a quiet place after I asked for forgiveness. That was my ah-ha moment! That was when I finally figured out what was different: I realized that I had just gotten an answered prayer! I was so giddy that I wanted to try something else and see if it worked on that too.

And when that happens to you, you will do just as I did and want to pray about something else that has been bothering you—and something else and something else. And before you know it, you will be enjoying talking to the Lord, and you will seek audiences with Him often. Why? Because you will love to pray, because you have been taught to love to pray. Above, I told you that I taught my students to want to learn by teaching them to love to learn. You, my friend, will have learned to want to pray because you learned to love to pray. Sounds strange, doesn't it? That's okay; it works!

When you get close to the Lord, you will find that that closeness nourishes your soul, and you will find yourself snuggling up to Him more and more, because to know Him is to love Him. You will find yourself receiving nourishment from your prayerful study of His word and your daily presence before His throne, for you have become a person who wants to pray because you have learned to love to pray.

- Make sure your life is free from sin. Always keep yourself in a condition that you not only can pray for yourself and others but that you actually *do* it.
- Don't forget the scripture that says that the "Prayers of the righteous availeth much" (James 5:16 KJV). Use the members of the church to help you through your Johnson grass or stormy times. Though they are chopping rows of their own, they will come together to help you if you ask. You are all in the field of cultivating souls, and they are working right alongside you.

- Ask the Father.
- Ask in belief.
- Ask in Jesus's name.
- Give your prayers power by showing love and praying for more than your family. Pray for the church leaders and the preacher, too. When was the last time you prayed for the church leaders, the church as a whole, and the church worldwide (James 5:16 KJV)?

R-U Ready?
The intention was to do it,
But trouble came before
I got to it.

Nothing in this world lies beyond the reach of prayer unless it is beyond the will of God. And one final thing: when you find yourself wondering why you are not bothered anymore, give the Lord thanks for an answered prayer, and spread the knowledge to your brother, sister, and neighbor. You will find that you have given them the tool to take their situation apart, analyze it, and come up with the same puzzled and wondrous summation that you did: though their problem is the same as it was an hour ago or yesterday, *they* are different! And uh oh! Suddenly, here are some more folks who have been taught to pray because they have learned to love to pray.

Then you will marvel at the love of God that upholds us in so many ways. You will find yourself and your neighbor, brother, sister, etc. stepping a little lighter because burdens don't seem so heavy. It is then that you know, my friend, that you have finally "let go and let GOD!" You have learned to love to pray, and you will never let go of that special bond you have developed with the Lord. You will yearn for quiet time so that you can tell Him, "Thank you." And you might even break out singing "There's a sweet relief in knowing, o-o-oh!... The LORD will make a way somehow!" Yes, every now and then, I break out in this song, whether I am in the midst of a storm or not, for you see, I want to praise Him because I have learned to love to praise Him! If we do this, the church will grow at the pace that it did during the days of Marshall Keeble, R. N. Hogan, and G. P. Bowser.

In conclusion, I hope you remember to utilize prayer and make it a part of your everyday life so that when you do have trouble, you don't have to worry about looking for the LORD. HE will know where you are, because you have established a fine relationship with HIM. HE will come to see about you if you just call; I know, for I have tried HIM.

Remember, too, that prayer didn't go out of business in biblical times, and God did not put a "Gone to Lunch" sign on the door during modern times. He is still in the prayer-answering business. (Read Hebrews 4:16.) I hope that this lesson blesses you today, but before I go I want to leave you with this brief poem of mine:

Grace and Faith

Riding on the clouds of joy one moment
And writhing in the clinging vines of despair the next,
Trying to make sense of all of the chaos
Before the twins of grace and faith
Arrive to disentangle and shepherd on to a higher loft

Prayer

Will remove you from "here" (disillusionment)
And help you to get to "there" (contentment)
Prayer

Renewal

Prayer renews my strength
Day by day
As I struggle to walk in
This Christian way.
When you have been in
Prayerful contact with God,
There is a serenity that holds you,
No matter where your footsteps may trod.
(excerpt from *DEI Sub Numine Viget*)

Pray

Went by the meeting house today
Went there to pray and give thanks
Came away from the meeting house today
A better person having gone to pray.
(excerpt from *DEI Sub Numine Viget*)

Today can be the tomorrow that you prayed about yesterday," so,
pray.

Discussion Questions

1. Have you checked over your life to see if you have reached your "one day?" if you have, thank Him again, and tell somebody about it. Brag on Him! What scripture lets us know that he likes that?

2. Do we always know when a prayer has been answered? Is it always immediate?

_____

3. What does it mean to learn to love to pray?

_____

_____

4. Is it "old-fashioned" to pray? Will prayer ever go out of style?

_____

_____

FOR FURTHER READING
Ephesians 5:20, James 5:16, 1 Thessalonians 5:16–18, Romans 8:26, Hebrews 5:7, Luke 18:10–14 KJV

Slights/Bullying (2 Corinthians 4:8-9 KJV)

§

AIM: To LEARN TO MAINTAIN Christian decorum when dealing with slights.

Song: "I've Been Picked Out to Be Picked On"

> Folks don't know what they do when they disturb the sheep
> That belong to the Shepherd,
> Who knows His sheep's every trembling bleat.

§

Often, hearts that are gentle and caring get trampled and abused, to be discarded like yesterday's refuse. Don't worry; waiting tells the story because it all comes out in the wash!

§

INTRODUCTION

Some people seem to toss out slights without any care or thought of the harm they might cause. Just what is a slight? Webster defines slight as an insult caused by a failure to show someone proper respect or attention; an affront; snub. In other words, to commit a slight is to go out of one's way to let someone know that he or she is thought of as a "nobody."

Slights can happen anywhere, but we tend to expect them to not occur among Christians. You would think that would be the case, but it is not. In this lesson, we are going to deal with slights coming from people in the workplace, school, and church by viewing some Cases in Point. People are people no matter where you go. In any given group, you will have a natural leader or leaders, depending upon the size of the group; a wannabe leader or leaders; and people who have self-concept problems.

People who have self-concept problems usually fall into two groups: the extremely quiet ones—oftentimes the victim—who hope to escape notice, or the vocal ones who want to call attention to someone else's shortcomings in hopes that their own will not be noticed.

You will find that in most groups, people gravitate toward the natural leader. You will also find a wannabe leader who is always striving for the approval of the leader. That person will usually hand out slights to others on a regular basis—especially to mousy persons who will not retaliate—in a conscious or unconscious drive for power such as is enjoyed by the leader.

SLIGHTS THAT COULD OCCUR ON THE JOB

Below are instances of slights that can occur on the job. We won't go into all of them, because time and ink do not permit:

* Having a boss who was given his position by his in-laws and who feels inadequate in the position because he deems others more qualified as he learns his new duties.
* Showing oneself to be gifted in doing a certain thing better than all comers (Nehemiah's situation).

* Showing oneself to be comfortable in one's own skin. In Nehemiah 4, we see that Nehemiah was a person of importance because he was cup bearer to the king. That could have been a reason he was targeted. He was of a different race. That could have been a reason he was targeted. No matter the reason, suffice it to say that when a person tries and fails to get to you with taunts and slights and ridicule, they will next try something worse. We can see that Sanballat and Tobiah got worse. After belittling the work being done on the wall did not work, they tried threats. When that didn't work, they planned a killing (Nehemiah 6:2). All through the process, Nehemiah kept working, praying, being vigilant, and steadily building the wall. Even when they sent for Nehemiah to come to discuss the situation, he didn't do it. His words were, "I can't come down." We need to use words to that effect when folks are trying to belittle us into stopping our work for the Lord. We need to answer as Nehemiah did: "I *cain't* come down." In Nehemiah's case, the end result was that the wall was built.

The situations mentioned above will cause a person to be targeted by the slighter in order to lower said person's perceived status in others' eyes. Their reasons for doing so may be multiple: jealousy, envy, or power hunger—or maybe they just get satisfaction out of destroying someone else, heathenism, etc.

SLIGHTS IN THE CHURCH

Have you ever met someone who was a Negative Nellie about everything and everybody, someone who never had anything good to say about anything or anyone? This type of personality usually shows up in church settings. These are people who do not have power anyplace else, so they *take* that power in religious settings. The Negative Nellie slighters will belittle, mock, discredit, spread gossip, lie, and insult others in any way they can to achieve a takedown in perceived status of a perceived challenger and an elevation in their own status—a "my way or the highway" attitude, if you will. These people often have the attitude of, "I run things *up in here.*" Here are a couple of examples they might use to employ their takedown skills:

- "Girl, have you heard...they tell me that she..."
- "I'm not spreading gossip, because it was in the paper, but girl, sit down..."
- "She thought she was looking so good with those last-season clothes on and her out-of-season shoes...and that hat. Everybody knows that you don't wear straw hats in the wintertime unless it is a polished straw! Child, please...and don't even get me started on..."

I want you to start thinking about how you would handle the situation if you came upon sisters discussing you in the ways mentioned above. We will get back to your answers in the section entitled "What to Do?" In the meantime, let's read a couple of cases in points.

1. **Case in Point**—Not too long ago, a situation arose in my life where I had to deal with a slight. That situation came about with the publishing of my book *W.O.W. created w.o.w.* Someone said, jokingly, that I had unrealistic optimism. They were referring to the wealth of encouragement and optimism that springs forth from the book. If you have not read it, then I encourage you to do so. It will bless you in ways that you might have taken for granted. **What Did I Do?**—Now, I could have taken that person's comment in the negative light intended, but I elected not to do that. Instead, I decided to accentuate that very quality in myself and make it a desirable attribute. I started becoming the Pollyanna that this lady had dubbed me. And now I get asked to speak to ladies' groups quite a bit. I figure that if I am going to be known for

something, then I might as well make sure it is positive and use it to the glory of the Lord. I quoted Isaiah 50:4 MSG, the scripture that talks about encouragers being put on this earth to do just that for the Lord. At this point in my life, I realized that the Lord was using me, yet again, according to His purpose. I had already become accustomed to chopping my row as a minister's wife for twenty-six years and wearing all the hats that you wear when you play that role. But what I had not counted on was being ridiculed about writing an encouraging book for my fellow man.

2. **Case in Point**—Not long after that slight, I received another slight concerning this same book, *W.O.W. created w.o.w.* One woman was bold enough to make a suggestion that she did not believe I wrote all of the material in the book. She told me she had said to her husband, "She did not write all of that, and I am going to ask her!" This second slight made me see two things: 1) the message I was trying to impart had been fully grasped by my readers, and 2) the Lord let me see myself as one who had done well what He had wanted me to do (Isaiah 50:4 MSG). **What Did I Do?**—I politely told her that through the Lord I had penned every word. Then I told her that if she saw me doing something well, she shouldn't attribute it to me, but to the glory of the Lord. Then she asked me how I did it. I asked her if she loved her family and her children, to which she answered in the affirmative. Then I asked her if she would go a whole day without speaking to her family. I told her that was the same situation I was in with my relationship with the Lord. I told her that because I love Him, I talk to Him in prayer. I told her that some of my most heartfelt poems are the result of my communing in prayer with Him. Then I quoted Isaiah 50:4 MSG to her. Read it for yourself.

3. **Case in Point**—Y'all know how bent out of shape a lot of us get when someone lies to us or bothers our children or

our mother. This last one is a bit long, but I made it long for a specific reason. I want you to gather the flavor of young Pete's dilemma; I want you to empathize or sympathize with him and realize once again that it is not always easy to behave as a Christian. Here we go:

Have you ever met a person who lies for the sake of lying? Lies to beat the band; lies, it seems, just to hear themselves talk? Whoo! I am coming on strong this morning; aren't I? Today we are going to meet Pete Handlebiz. How about that last name hmm? Tee hee, I couldn't resist mentioning it. Anyway, Pete is the type of person who shoots straight as an arrow and does not tolerate much foolishness.

"Enough!" yelled Pete. Everybody got quiet. The boys got quiet, and his sister stopped flipping channels on the TV. His brothers decided that neither one of them wanted the toy tank they had built together and had been fighting over. It lay in the floor forgotten. Nobody moved much when Pete used that voice. They all knew that he would start separating bodies and hitting next. Pete said, "Julie, go set the table for dinner. Bob (short for Robert), go change the cat-litter box, and I'd better not smell it when I come in there. And don't be slinging litter everywhere. If you spill some, get it up. Joe, unwind the dog chain and give him fresh water. And when you come back in here, bring a book to read, all of you, since it is summertime and you don't have any homework."

They all scooted to do as Pete bade, except Julie. She just stood there. Pete was forced to look up from the help-wanted ads he had been scanning. He ran his hand through his hair and asked, "What now, Julie?"

Julie sidled across the worn beige carpet and said, "When I come back from setting the table, instead of reading, can I bring my crocheting kit that Mrs. Branson gave me?"

"Yeah, that's fine," Pete said.

Pete remembered back to the time in his life when he did not have to ride herd on his siblings. But that was before his daddy died. He no longer was that talkative eight-year-old that everyone used to jostle each other to sit next to. He had become a quiet and serious-minded sixteen-year-old. His outlook on life had changed when he had had to take on the task of helping his mom raise his siblings. Before his daddy died, Pete would often hear his mother tell his younger brothers and sometimes his sister, "Just wait 'til your daddy comes home. He'll see to you!" He used to wonder why she didn't just spank them and be done with it, because they were always good for almost two weeks after his daddy spanked them. But she never did; she always waited for his daddy. And since Daddy was gone, it had become Pete's job.

Pete finished scanning the local want ads. He had been hoping to find summer jobs for the boys. Pete was thankful for the job delivering flowers three days a week. Still, it would help if he got something that paid more money or offered more hours per week. Yet, he didn't complain. He knew that having the delivery job was a blessing, because he could drop by to check on the boys and his sister if he needed to, and he saved money on lunch that way too. He sighed and was still contemplating the job situation when Julie came back in, lugging her crocheting box. She had been given a small kit, but Julie's work had soon needed more space and had grown to fruit-box size, though Julie, bless her heart, still referred to it as her kit.

Julie placed her things just so around her and then bent to get the ripple afghan she had just started. From upstairs, she had drug her granny-square throw from her bedroom chair and her crochet on the double afghan that she had made for her bed.

"Pete," eleven-year-old Julie said.

Pete looked up. "What, Julie?"

"I was wonderin' if I could make some throws and coverlets for some of my friends and all."

Pete had learned years before never to take anything Julie asked him for granted, so he said, "And just what does 'and all' mean?"

"Well," said Julie, sort of hem-hawing. "I wondered if I might sell some of them in the children's bazaar booth at the July Fourth and Labor Day picnics?"

Pete looked at Julie, his little sis, and wondered where the time had gone. He couldn't believe that she was eleven years old. It seemed just yesterday that Dad had died. Pete shook himself out of his reverie and replied, "I don't know, Julie, let me ask Mom about that. Okay?"

Julie said, "I hate it when you say that, because you and Mom always say no to everything I want to do to help out around here. In case you both hadn't noticed, I am not a baby anymore. When Daddy died, he didn't leave no babies!"

Pete pushed back from the table and reached Julie in one stride. He enfolded her in his arms and said, "Aww, Punkin, that's not fair."

Julie started to cry and told him about the girls in her English class talking about where they would be doing school shopping during the summer. She told Pete that Gwendolyn Braggadocious had listed all of the girls in the room that mattered. After she had done that to the whispering snickers and thumbs-up from her buddies, she had proceeded to name the other girls in the room one by one. She had said that Hanna Ship was too fat to matter. The whole class had laughed at that. "But I didn't laugh, because I did not think it was funny, and I wondered what she was going to say when she got to me," said Julie.

Pete was wiping his sister's eyes when the boys came in from their chores, books in hand. They both stopped in the kitchen doorway and chorused, "What's wrong with Julie?"

"Nothing a little family talk and TLC won't cure," Pete said roughly.

Joe bounded into the room and grabbed a tissue out of the tissue box on the table and handed it to his sister before settling himself on the sofa. Bob sat in the wingback chair that Momma always used.

"All right, guys, Mom just drove up in the driveway, so go help her bring in the food," said Pete.

The boys bounced up and headed toward the glassed-in area that was their front porch. Then they stopped short. Their mom was already out of the car, and she was hurriedly wiping her eyes as she turned away from the windows back toward the car. Bob, ever the sharp one, said, "She looks like she's been crying."

They both turned and went back into the living room, and Joe said to Pete, "Momma's been crying. Shh."

When Momma came into the front room, four innocent-looking pair of eyes were intently looking at her. She said to Julie, "Where's my hug; can't a momma get a hug around here today?" To which all of her children responded, and she ended up in a big bear of a group hug.

Julie's voice was heard from within the group hug. "Momma, why were you crying?"

The boys yelled, "Julie!"

Momma shushed each one of them and told them all to sit down. Then she said, "I have some bad news, children."

Bob piped up, "I hope it don't mean that I don't get my X-box for my birthday."

Pete cleared his throat and grunted under his breath and said, "What is it, Momma, that has made you cry?"

"It's nothing that a little extra effort from all of us won't remedy. It's just that Claudia Braggadocious used my computer after hours yesterday and sent out some unflattering emails about the boss's wife. The boss's wife came to the office today, and we all could hear her crying from his office. When she left, she gave me a red-eyed, malevolent stare and hissed as she passed me that she had been nothing but good to me. Then her husband called me into his office and fired me after yelling at me. He was so mad when he called me in that he slammed his office door so hard that it bounced back open, and all of the office got to hear him dress me down. I was so humiliated that I could not hold my head up as I packed my things."

Momma sat down on the arm of the couch, finished drying her tears, and said, "But that is that. What we have to do is figure out how to make ends meet until I can get another job. Pete, I didn't stop by the store on my way home. Do you kids think that you can eat the remainder of yesterday's spaghetti for dinner?"

"Sure we can, can't we, troop?" said Joe.

When Momma headed to the bathroom to freshen up, Pete, who had not said a word, looked at Bob and said, "You are in charge until

I get back. Make sure everybody gets the same amount of spaghetti. Me? Don't worry about me. I ate on the truck today."

Pete went upstairs and came back down with his steel baseball bat and banged out the door. He was muttering under his breath about seeing a liar about a lie and a bonehead about a bone.

Momma came out of the bathroom to see him tearing down the road in her car. All she could do was wring her hands, because she had never learned to drive their other car, that old stick of Pete's that had belonged to her husband. Momma got on the phone and called her brother, Justin, in Toledo, two hundred miles away.

Now ladies, I bet somebody is sitting there thinking, "Oh boy! What is he going to do? Lawd have mercy; I hope he don't let them get him *into* trouble!"

Have you ever known someone to be in the grips of justifiable anger, like Pete is in? I'm pretty sure you have. My question to you is, "What's he going to do with that bat?!" Oh my, this youngster has his whole life ahead of him. Oh dear! Oh dear! Gotcha going, don't I? Well, keep reading, and let's see what happens.

Pete was so angry that he could see red. He was angry with his dad for dying; he was angry with Claudia Braggadocious and her snooty daughter; he was angry at life for making a sixteen-year-old do a man's job; but most of all, he was angry with Benny Grabrun for firing his mother without checking the facts.

Pete thought about the last time he had seen red. That had been years ago, about a week after his dad's funeral. His brother Bob had sassed his mother something awful because she had told him for the fifteenth time to turn his television off and go to sleep. When he had refused, his mom had marched into the boys' room and had yanked the TV cord out from the wall so hard that it had bent the prong on the plug.

That was when Bob, probably because he was grieving, had said that he hated her. His mom had replied, "Join the club; life hates me too." Pete would always remember the way his mom had run past his room, sobbing. Pete remembered that he had said out loud, "Daddy, why did you go and leave us like this?" He had lain in his bed listening to his mom sobbing. When things had gotten quiet in her room, Pete had made a pretend trip to the bathroom. When he tiptoed past his mom's room, he could hear the quiet, even sound of her breathing. Every now and then she would hiccup in her sleep.

Pete had been on his way back to his room when he saw light coming from under his brothers' door. Pete had opened the door and had seen Bob watching TV. Pete had said to Bob, "You turn that TV off right now, and if you ever make my mom cry again, I will beat you up within an inch of your life." Bob had said, "You ain't my dad." Pete saw red! Before he realized what he was doing, he had hit his brother with a round-off kick and knocked him down, and had his knee pressing against Bob's windpipe. That had been when Joe, who had been quietly watching the whole thing, had jumped up and said, "Pete, 'top it, 'top! You gonna git 'im dead!"

Pete had let Bob up. Then he had said to Bob, "The TV stays off for a week. You got me? And if you ever make Momma cry again, I'll beat you, Bob, and you know I can!" Joe scurried to turn the TV off. Bob, who had been gasping for breath, said, "She my momma, too." To that Pete snarled, "Then act like it."

Pete had vowed then that he would never lose his temper like that again, and he never had. He had never seen red again until today.

While clenching the metal bat, he gunned the car through the traffic light that had just turned red...

§

Remember, I told you at the beginning of the third Case in Point that it was not always easy to behave as a Christian, but we have to remember that it is possible. It becomes a bit easier the more you practice it. So, no matter how justifiable your anger seems, you cannot go running off the way Pete did. Or can you? Did Pete sin? How would you handle the situation as a Christian? (The rest of Pete Handlebiz's story can be read in the soon-to-be-released book, *The Victor's Song*.)

What Would You Do?—You might be asking, "What do you do in situations like this?" Remember, I told you always to begin your day with prayer. Then practice that very thing. I also find that it is helpful to call the offender's name in your prayer. Nothing harmful or detrimental, mind you! Just a sincere prayer that the person leaves you alone so you can do your job, that the person will look upon you with favor, or that you be moved to a team or department so that you are no longer answerable to him or her. Prayers of that sort seem to work. It worked in Nehemiah's case. I do know that if the person rides you too much, you will get to see him or her be dealt with by a bigger dog with a bigger bite. If you are prayerful and faithful, this usually is the case (Esther 5:14; 7:10).

However, under no circumstances are you to allow that person to get you to behave like an infidel (a person who does not know the LORD), because then people will always be looking for the next thing they can do to you, especially if you show that their taunts and barbs bother you. Whatever you do, you can't let the frustration build up in you until it explodes. Keep it prayed down.

The following poem of mine sums it up nicely for us:

> You have to leave yesterday's slights far behind.
> Today is a new day for you to exercise
> To your fellowman the art of being kind.
>
> What seemed like a slight yesterday
> Might have been the deciding factor that
> Caused beneficent eyes to turn your way.

Live your life like you know that God is able. That means putting on a brave face and having well-worn knees. It means that in trying times, you can act in a way that surprises the rest of the world. And when you do, you will amaze people with your faith and trust in the Lord. And you know what else you will be doing without even realizing it? You will be doing what I always liken the Christian life to:

> Chopping and weeding your row,
> As fruit for God, you try to grow.

Peace on the outside comes from knowing God on the inside.

Now, my make-believe story may seem impossible, but some people really do interact in our lives this way. Some people can be so callous in their regard for us or our feelings that we feel a strong need for revenge. They make us see red! That is when we have to take a chill pill. Read this next paragraph, and you will see what I mean.

"Even the very hairs of your head are all numbered!" (Luke 12:7 KJV) That means you are so precious to God that wherever you go and in whatever situation you find yourself, He goes with you. And He is the Shepherd that guards you, His sheep! Woo! Those are some powerful words, but you know, folks, we sometimes need powerful reminding of Who we say we serve. We talked about prayer in lesson 8, so let's put it to use starting now. Pray for those who are mistreated the world over. If you are one who is being slighted, then pray for the offenders to be at peace with you; call their names in your prayers; pray that either of you be moved to a different branch at work; pray that they leave you alone so you can do your job; pray that they look upon you with favor, etc. Prayers of this sort seem to work.

Never allow situations to sour you on people or on life. Instead, use each day to go forth and heal some wounded spirits by showing love.

> Forgiving is moving past pain
> To being able to breathe again
> And looking at life without viewing
> It through a jaundiced pane.

Find someone less fortunate than you today, and give him or her a big smile or a handshake. You just might be the one to break the chain in that person's cycle of being slighted, ignored, or put down. All of us have suffered slights of some sort or another. You remember how bad you felt when that happened to you. So, let us put ourselves in the shoes of someone less fortunate or less popular and extend kindness. It costs you nothing and could gain you plenty. Let us make sure that we are not the one who causes someone to whisper brokenly to themselves, "That person hurt my feelings."

So, to all of you, but especially to those of you who are put down on a regular basis, remember that God loves you, and so do I—and the Lord looks upon us all the same.

> Sometimes people will look for
> Excuses to not like you at all,
> And they often wish with all their hearts
> To see you take a fall.

About me, people often say
"She thinks she is **so much**!"
But what those people do not know
Or just plain fail to see
Is the fact that what they perceive
As arrogant independence is
Jesus's touch in me.

See the beautiful bird in all its fine plumage? Well, just you remember that the very hairs of your head are numbered! He sees your pain, anguish, and mistreatment; he sees the ditches dug for you, etc. "Be still and know." And then step on in His name, blessed one. Step on.

When a person is overlooked, it usually means they do not have much of a social status. This practice, though forbidden, has been going on since biblical times. James 2:1, 4, and 8 KJV tells us to treat people without partiality. We are not to make people feel bad because of their lack of social status. We are told to love others as we do ourselves. Y'all know that we do not neglect ourselves, and we get upset if someone else does. Then let us treat all people nicely. You never know who you are talking to, whether you are being mean or being kind. Remember the words "angels unawares" (Hebrews 13:2 KJV).

§

Not Much

It does not take much
To have a loving touch.
Just do to and for your fellowman
What you would do or want to be done for yourself
If you found yourself in situations as such.

§

Peas in a Pod

Why be unkind to the person
That you meet?
Why tear them down to such
An extent that they can scarce
Stay on their feet?

For all men are like peas in a pod
And will have the pod cover of clay
Peeled back one day
And reveal every footstep you made
To show every soul for whom or against
Whom you did trod.

§

Discussion Questions

1. What was Sanballat and Tobiah's reason for wanting to stop the rebuilding of the wall?

2. Name a scripture illustrating how we should react to the Sanballats and Tobiahs of today.

3. What would your reaction be to two sisters you happened to overhear discussing you and/or your family in a very negative light?

4. What is meant by the green-box insert that "It all comes out in the wash?" Cite a scripture that means the same thing.

5. What are some reasons that people slight or bully others?

   What should be our response when we see this happening?

6. In the poem "Peas in a Pod," what is meant by the peeling back of the pod cover one day?

For Further Reading

Esther 5:14, 7:10; Isaiah 41:10–13; Romans 12:14; 1 Corinthians 16:14; Psalm 34:19; Psalm 91; Psalm 23; John 10:28–30; Matthew 12:36; Proverbs 19:11 KJV

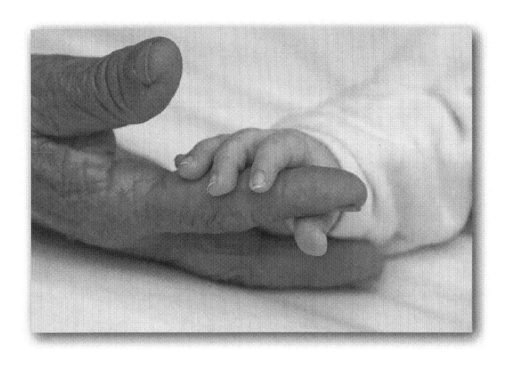

Grandma's Hands (Psalm 78:2-4 KJV)

§

AIM: To REALIZE THE IMPACT that we as ladies have on the cultivation of, retention of, and encouragement of souls.

Song: "Grandma's Hands"

INTRODUCTION

We often hear ladies complain—and probably do some complaining ourselves—about how limited we are in what we **can** do. Ladies, I don't think we realize just how big the responsibility is that we **do** have. You have heard it said, "The hand that rocks the cradle rules the world." That is so true. We have the responsibility of the future church in our hands. That means we need to be guarded in every-thing we say and do. We need to be mindful of the fact that children and babes are watching and emulating us.

That means people are watching us and wanting to be just like us. We have taken on protégées and do not realize it, most of us. No, we most likely did not willingly take on these protégées, but they are there nevertheless. Still not quite getting what I am saying? If you make a habit of going to the club and drinking and talking about what a great time you had, etc., people out there are listening to you and saying in their mind, "Oh, so we can still go to the club and have fun; that's good to know! I'm going next Friday night, and I am going to be dressed to the nines." Maybe you are so smooth that you electrify people with your moves on the dance floor. Mmm hmm, there is somebody that wants to be just like you. There is a mini "wannabe you" walking around just waiting for the right time and opportunity.

We often make the mistake of thinking that only children will emulate us, but that is not the case. The world and babes in Christ are watching us, too. If you live to be a hundred, you can never do all that has been laid on your plate to do. Since you know that people are watching you and that your every gesture will be copied, do be careful in what you say and do.

Before my husband became a preacher, I did not bother myself much with what people thought. I was my own person, had my own plans, and was moving right along with them. But oh, when he became a preacher, resentment built up, and I resisted the thought that I could not be my own person anymore! I looked upon myself as an adult, and I figured I was not going to bend and give way just so other people could have their way or feel good, unnecessarily, about their opinion. I was a person, and I had opinions, too. I *wutten stuttin' 'em!* (meant so little to me that I never gave it a second thought)

But little did I know! I was grousing to myself one day that I did not have a decision in this matter. Nobody asked me what I thought. If I had wanted a preacher, I would have married a preacher! When I got awakened to the reality that this man was the Lord's servant and that I, as his wife, was supposed to help him, I still resented the fact. How was I awakened to the previous fact? Easy: we had an elderly neighbor whom I respected highly, and she sat me down and told me. I remember shedding tears quietly as she talked to me.

When I got back home, I went to my knees, and I began to talk to the Lord. I told Him that He knew that I was not preacher-wife material, because my temper was too quick. I told Him that I did not know how to do it. I told Him that since He had been with me all my life and since I knew that, I would do what it seemed that I was supposed to do, even though I did not want to do it. After a few more tears, I asked Him to show me how to be a good preacher's wife. I started watching our current preacher's wife and how she handled things. I soaked up all that she did. I weighed out her decisions in my mind and chose the wisest of them to emulate.

A few months later, when my husband was asked to be the minister of a small congregation, I was ready and prepared—at least I thought I was. (Read more about my lack of being prepared in lesson 13.) Armed with the Lord, I went boldly on.

Use your talents to glorify Him.

How and Why

You never know how far-reaching your touch on someone's life will be. So, be cautious and loving when you do touch. Think about it… In my blog (Quipsbyalma.blogspot.com) for June 6, I wrote a piece entitled "Pause for Station Identification." Why did I entitle it as I did? Here's why. Back in the days of radios, the announcer used to pause for station identification. That meant that the announcer wanted to remind you where you were (i.e., that you were on their particular station). This blog was entitled as it was for that day, to remind us all where we are, why we are here, and what we are supposed to be doing.

As mothers, grandmothers, cousins, aunts, and sisters, we need to think of the impact we could have on people's lives. Somebody's always watching how we chop our row!

Training the Church of Tomorrow

It is all of our jobs to train the next generation. And we know that children will do things they ought not to do, especially if their parents are not around. How do we know this? We know what we did as children, plus the Bible pretty much says it, too. Here are a couple of scriptures to consider: Proverbs 22:6 and Psalm 78:1–8 KJV. In short, my blog piece from June 6 was written to remind us that though we are here now, this is only a temporary situation. We are leaving; how have we prepared the church of tomorrow to carry on?

We Want to Help

We are leaving here every day
So let us leave something behind
In our leaving, from our living.

One last tidbit to share with all.
Don't you remember when you were
A child and some adult who was not your
Mom or dad saved you from doing something bad?

And now you look back on those days
With a joyful sense of relief.
Then we too must be that beckoning beacon
Of safety to help today's youth
Who need guidance just as much
As we did, and that my friend
Is the truth
If it ever were to be told.
We have to help save children from themselves,
For under some of that dross is gold.

Again, Mom, we stick our noses
Where they don't belong,
Because many a child has been
Saved from following the path labeled "Wrong"
By a meddling old busybody who
Would not leave other folks' children alone.
And we can step a little lighter
In knowing that we have handed
Our batons to sound-minded souls
And that all will be well when we are all gone.

Somebody told us and we told you
And we're thankful for the "old busybodies"
Who helped us make it through,
For the voice of reason often whispers
"Had it not been for them, just think
What would have happened to you?"

We are leaving here every day,
So let us leave something behind
In our leaving, from our living.

JUST SAYIN'...

A child does not know the right way, because he is too young in the ways of the world. But we know, and it is our responsibility to train the church of tomorrow. I remember when I used to quote my elders and say, "The old folks say..." when I was trying to make a valid point to my peers. Then one day it hit me. I cannot say that anymore, because I have become one of the old folks! That was a sobering thought, let me tell you.

Then I got to thinking. What have I done with this life that I have? What legacy am I leaving behind? Have I tried to help any person who came my way, whether it was child or not? Or did I do as so many do today and keep the kind of hands-off policy I have heard so many speak about: "Child, you better not bother that little boy or little girl! You will have his momma all over you! These young folks nowadays don't want you saying nothing to their children. I have learned my lesson, honey; if it is not me or mine, I keep my nose out of it! These kids nowadays are something else, and their mommas too."

What if the old folks back in my days of youth had turned a blind eye to some of the things I got into when I was a child? Now, I will admit that unlike some of our mothers of today, my mother encouraged the older ladies in the community to keep an eye out for us, for which I am now thankful, but I was not then, let me tell you. But ladies, that is no excuse, now is it? I mean, if I get set out by someone because I corrected her child in a loving manner, then so be it. The Bible tells us, "Foolishness is bound up in the heart of a child" (Proverbs 22:15 KJV).

Children don't know what is coming up in the cruelty of this world, but we do, by the mere fact that we have been living a number of years. We can teach and talk from experience. The time will come when that child is going to need to reach for a higher power.

Young Mothers

If you have not taken your children to worship services and let them see you practicing what they hear the preacher saying, you may lose them to the pull of the world. If they saw you going to the club on Friday or Saturday, even if you go to a club out of town, they know. You are training a soul. I never will forget a lady who came to me in tears because her child, whom she idolized, told her that she could not reprimand her, because she was bumping on the dance floor every weekend just like she was. Yep, she had always been one of those mothers who said, "Do what I say, not what I do." And yes, it came back to bite her.

Remember the adage that "Children learn what they live." I am happy to say that this mother got the chance to turn her life around, and she got to hear her children commend her for it. Never forget that when God allowed you to have that baby, He gave you a soul to train for one of two armies, God's or the adversary's. You don't have to choose which army; just do nothing and you will have already made your choice, because the world will make it for you.

Young mothers, when we read Proverbs in the fourth paragraph of the beginning section, I was by no means advocating someone putting hands on your child. But a few well-chosen words would not be amiss. There is an old African proverb that says, "It takes a village." That means use the eyes and ears of everyone you can, because children are going to get away with as much as they can; it is just in their nature. That baby or child who you love too much to have someone say a stern word to may cause you to howl with regret one day. Which would you rather see:

1. Stern words, or having your child "blessed" into a gang by being beat almost senseless
2. Stern words, or having your child locked up to suffer beatings by the jailor or assaults by other inmates
3. Stern words, or having that child sentenced on a capital-murder charge
4. Stern words, or having that child strung out on the latest dope, with little or no hope
5. Stern words, or having that child become a prostitute or a call girl

There are several other things I could mention in this vein, but I think I have said enough to give you something to think about. Note: Young mothers, keep your children with you at the worship services if you don't want anyone saying anything to them. And teach them respect for the edifice, their elders, the church leaders, their teachers, etc. Most of all, teach them respect for God, and remember that we can help you if you let us.

Case in Point—In my last year of a thirty-year teaching career, a parent verbally accosted me about the difficulty of the work I had the children doing and about my strict grading. She told me that people were talking and that she was just going to be honest and straight up with me. She said she was not going to talk behind my back. She emphatically told me I needed to curve my grades. It was a pretty heated exchange from her end and stunned silence from mine. I could not get a word in edgewise.

Now, mind you, I was one of the most lenient teachers in my building. It was said that if you could not pass my class, then you must have gone to class and just slept. That parent came to me at the end of the six weeks and apologized, and she did so again several years later. She told me she realized that my class was very easy compared to some of the college classes her child was struggling through. Numerous kids have come back to me and thanked me for the structure of my class, because it prepared them for harder classes later and for college. Some even use some of the methods that I used in my classes. I said all of that to say this: If someone comes down hard on your child for whatever reason, talk it out with the child and smooth it over, but don't always look for the easy way out for him or her. It may be a preparation for life.

And whatever you do, get the whole story. The parent mentioned above had not found out from her child that she was failing my class simply because she refused to do expounded definitions. If you turned in all the assignments, you automatically got 100. Her child had decided it was too hard and too much work and she was not going to do it. And get this—even if you did not turn in anything but one out of fifteen of the assigned words with a definition, the lowest grade I would give was a 69, which at the time was one point from passing!

Foolishness bound up in the heart of a child is proven again. Don't be so quick to believe what the child says in its entirety. Most will say anything to keep from being grounded. And above all, remember we are available to help.

Biblical Case in Point Combined with Secular—We all know the story of Jezebel and what a wicked woman she was. Well, I want to compare her influence to the Mississippi River. The Mississippi River begins from Lake Itasca in Minnesota as a trickle so small that you can stand with one foot on one bank and the other foot on the opposite bank. It ends up being called the mighty father of waters as it makes its cascading run down toward the ocean to meet the churning waters of the Gulf of Mexico. On its run to the sea, it often tears trees from their banks and stones from places where they have long been set, and it churns rocks, pebbles, and sand on toward its mouth, or delta. It changes the landscape wherever it meanders. Sometimes on its turbulent trip to the sea, it overflows its banks and sweeps unsuspecting people and things into its wake. As it nears its mouth, it further changes the landscape by depositing some of the trees, rocks, soil, and other debris at its mouth or delta. Yet some of the debris is hurled headlong into the ocean. Still, it all begins with a tiny trickle.

- Would you say that this example is a good way of illustrating the adage that trouble is easy to get into but difficult to get out of, in that the river was easily handled or crossed at the beginning? At that point, it is not a problem to hop from one bank to the other. There's no danger of being swept in. People often walk that little trickle and stand in it with water not even covering their shoes. How easy it is to navigate it—sort of like someone saying of trouble, "No problem, I got this." Ya think?

"Jezebel's reign began with that first act of cruelty, of power, of dominance. We don't know what that first act on her road to being eaten by dogs was. We just know that she took it. Had she not, then she would not have become known as the evil influence that she was. Her practices, whatever they were, influenced her children, too" (Deen, 125–131). Just think; that first despicable act started a legacy of terror that swept to and through her children to reach all the way to you and yours. Yep, you heard me correctly: all the way to you and yours. You ask me, "How?" In no situation in modern times have I ever heard of anyone naming a child Jezebel, have you? You see—that is exactly what I meant. Her name became so synonymous with evil that no mother would dare give her little girl that name. Yet, it started with just a trickle...

* Wonder if she would have changed her ways if she knew the evil that the mere mention of her name would symbolize for all time?
* Wonder if she would have changed her ways if she knew that the dogs would actually eat her? Somebody might be thinking, "She did know, because Elisha warned her." Well, not really, according to her frame of mind. You see, she felt he caused a cataclysmic injury to her kingdom, so she intended to deliver one back. She felt she was so powerful that she had the power to show Elisha just who he was dealing with. Her God was Baal, and she was determined to do away with Elijah and deliver a final blow to the servants of Yahweh. Because she had gotten away with killing so many prophets before, she thought she could do it again. You know, there are some people who act the same way. They get by for so long that they lose sight of Who is really in charge. It started with just a small trickle… Wonder if Jezebel would have changed? Well, we know what the rich man tried to do from his fiery prison, don't we? Yep, he wanted to do personal work in the form of keeping his brothers from having to come to that place of torment.

Whether we occupy the role of mother, grandmother, aunt, cousin, in-law, sister, or friend, let us be mindful of the role we have and never worry about the things we are not allowed to do; it is enough if we perform the awesome task that we *have* been given to do. For not only has Jezebel shown us, but secular history has too. In court records and church history, we have been shown and are still being shown that our influence in the lives of others is of paramount importance. There goes the momma, then her son or daughter, then the son's children, the daughter's children, the children's children, and so forth. Here are a few examples:

- Generations of nonworking individuals, robbers, and killers
- Generations of preachers, deacons, song leaders, and other church leaders
- Generations of preacher's wives, Sunday-school teachers, and other faithful and caring sisters

Remember that it is not just about you.

It is important that we build people's faith by letting them see our faith in action when the waters of trouble roll by. We should let them hear us say through all of our difficulties, as Sister S. E. Hampton, late of Milan, Tennessee, always said, "I declare; He will make everything all right!" We can further:

- build people's faith by our reaction to sickness.
- build people's faith by our reaction when people talk about us.
- build people's faith by our reaction when folks lie on us.
- build people's faith by our reaction when enemies connive against us.
- build people's faith by rejoicing when He does deliver us, by being so jubilant we share the news far and wide. My Gran Gran used to say that we needed to do this, to such an extent that people will copy our example, and catchphrases such as "I declare; He will make it all right" that those catchphrases will become a part of their lives as well,
- build people's faith by doing whatever positive thing we can while we can.

Ladies, whether or not we are elderly, we set an example, so let's remember that when we want to barbeque the preacher, the elders, the leading brothers, or other sisters, we are influencing someone.

We are building the legacy that will live on long after our voices have been silenced. What a great legacy to have:

* Because we went to Bible study, somebody else did too.
* Because we went to worship, somebody else did too.
* Because we visited the sick, somebody else did too.
* Because we studied our Bibles, somebody else did too.
* Because we put Christ first in all we said and did, somebody else did too.

Eternity. You, me, and our posterity. We are the examples; it's as simple as that. Think about it.

Church of Tomorrow

A little child watched me
A middle schooler, and a teenager did too,
As through life, I made my way.
What did I teach them by my actions each day?

Church of tomorrow is being built by you.
What are you building for young folks
By the things they see you do?

Do you practice charity
In your daily living,
Or are you too busy
Trying to make a buck
To be bothered with the
Practice of teaching giving?

Not about things I acquire,
Not about things I desire,

Not about things as all
About readying the next generation
To answer the gospel's call.

§

Granny

There is a sweet old lady
That I know
Who is known as Granny
Wherever she goes.

Sister S. E. Hampton is
Who I am talking about;
She's a hard church worker
And is very devout.

She sets a good example
For us women to go by,
While sending up timbers for
Her mansion on high.

Though she has a loving family
That she cherishes, you can tell,
Granny's love is all-encompassing
And includes her church, as well.

She takes the time to counsel
When you need a friend,
And she gives good advice
Time and time again.

So, my goal on my Christian
Journey is to be
A really faithful, hard worker
Just like Granny.
(excerpt from *DEI Sub Numine Viget*)

When I looked at her, I saw a rare jewel, and I have patterned my Christian walk after the love and wisdom I found there. What better legacy can there be?

Each of us is building a legacy of our own. We need to think about what we want read when all has been said and all has been done. When time bumps one final time into eternity, what do we want to be read?

Discussion Questions

1. If a new family with several unruly small children has just started attending your church, should anything be said or done if the children walk all over the newly cushioned pews?

   _____

2. Why is it important for us to be careful in everything we say and do?

   _____

   _____

3. We are teaching when we don't realize that children are being taught. Explain.

   _____

   _____

4. Do you think Jezebel would have changed her ways if she knew the dogs would really eat her? Are there people of the same deep mindset today when it comes to doing wrong?

For Further Reading
Deuteronomy 6:5, 11:19 KJV

LESSON 11

Writing It Down (Deuteronomy 4:9-10, Jeremiah 9:24 NKJ)

AIM: To REALIZE THE VALUE in writing a journal that will still speak long after our voices have gone still. They are tender touches to span time and generations of families simultaneously.

Song: "Mansion, Robe, and Crown"

Lessons within a Detoured Path

Traveling the path of others long gone
With detours thrown in so that I make it my own,
Leaving a trail through uncharted ground
So that by tomorrow's pilgrim it can be found.

Pilgrim of tomorrow, of this be aware:
The path we made for you is sure,
But detours are necessary to build
Your strength so that you endure
And carve a path with your own signature.
Always be mindful of your tomorrow's pilgrim,
Who is eager to begin his journey on life's thoroughfare.

Writing It All Down

Speaks to my soul
Brings me joy
Makes my heart sing
And makes my bells of contentment ring
As encouraging and inspiring words
To mine and other's posterity I bring.

INTRODUCTION

Though the Bible tells us that we are epistles read of men, oftentimes we are still surprised when it is called to our attention that someone is patterning his or her life after the example we set. Such a statement makes us uncomfortable at times, doesn't it? But we are giving to the church, which will be here after we are gone, words to use as tools for handling situations that may come up from time to time. This book will be one such tool at hand as they make their way in this world. How do I know this? I know because sometimes, in my life, it helps to recall those conversations I had with a wise loved one who has gone on. But there are so many folks who may not have given heed to or even had the opportunity to sit under the tutelage of a wise one. For that reason, I wrote some things down.

Case in Point—Something my momma told me when I was just eight years old had such an impact upon me that it continues to impact my life, even to this day. What thing is this? Listen, and put yourself in the mind of an eight-year-old, okay? You can do it—just humor me a bit, will you?

If you have ever had the privilege of indulging in a good fairytale, then you realize the euphoric cloud that I walked home under one particular day when I was eight years old. This would be the day that our teacher introduced us to the children's story "Jack and the Beanstalk." On any given day, it was my mother's habit to ask us what we had learned or done at school that day.

The clip art of a beanstalk that I have included for you is to help put you in the mind of a naïve, endearing little third grader. Yes, I was an optimistic little soul, and a caring, tender-hearted one at that.

One this particular day, I skipped until I got tired, walked for a bit, and started skipping again. Now mind you, I had three miles to go, but that did not bother me. I hopped, skipped, and played on my way home from school, as I did most days. I could not wait to get home to tell my momma what I had learned in school that day. And you know what else? I knew that today was extra special, because today was Tuesday—Momma's day off. That meant I would get to smell the hot food she would have waiting for me and my brothers. There would be baked sweet potatoes with a small amount of margarine, maybe neck bones and Irish potatoes, or pinto beans and pig's ears. Then again, I knew there was the chance that we might be having black-eyed peas. Yuck! Neither I nor my brothers liked black-eyed peas, but Momma said they were good for us.

When I got home, I walked through the door, and I could smell what smelled like neck bones and potatoes...and I smelled something else. It smelled like cake! Had Momma baked a cake? I walked through the corridor of the front room, the middle room, the hall, the dining room, and at last to the kitchen. Yes! There sat a cake on the table. I went out the back door looking for my mother and found her talking with my aunt who lived upstairs. I walked up to Momma and took from her the clothes she had just taken from the line.

By the time I heard the back-door slam, I had changed into my play-clothes and had hung up my school clothes. Momma told me to wash my hands and come to the table to eat. I kept up incessant chatter while I washed my hands with the Octagon soap, until Momma said, "You pay attention to what you are doing so you get your hands clean. You can tell me about school after you get your plate and sit down at the table."

"Yes, ma'am," I said in a subdued voice.

When I got my food and sat back down at the table, Momma said, "Okay, so tell me what has you so excited that you could hardly get in the door before you told me?"

I said, "In reading group today, our teacher read us a new story. It was called 'Jack and the Beanstalk.'"

"Okay, tell Momma the story."

I launched into the story using my best storytelling voice, just as I had heard Momma do many times. When I finished the story, with Jack getting an ax and chopping the beanstalk down, Momma was giggling, and her eyes shone with motherly love and pride.

She patted me on the back and got up to cut the cake. "I don't suppose you are too excited to eat a bit of cake, are you?"

"Nooo ma'am, I can't never be that excited, Momma!"

§

So, that night when it was storytelling time, I begged my momma to tell us the story of "Jack and the Beanstalk." When she finished, I sat back with a blissful sigh, as I always did when Momma finished whatever story she was telling us. Still in the grips of the blissful storybook moment, I said to Momma, "Momm-uh! Wouldn't it be good if magic beans were real?"

Oh, the scoffing laughter that burst forth from my brothers. "Ha ha ha ha! Man, are you dumb! There's no such thing as magic beans! You're so stupid! Ha ha ha ha!"

To that, Momma replied, "Leave your sister alone, boys. And yes, it would be nice, but that's only in fairy tales. All right, everybody! Scoot! Off to bed, you guys."

§

The next day, Momma sat me down and told me she needed to talk to me. She gave me that penetrating stare that seemed to look through me. I didn't like it when my momma looked at me like that, because most of the time it meant I was in trouble or she was about to tell me something serious.

Momma said, "Beanstalk magic is not real, but there is something better that is. That something is prayer and Jesus. You know how

Momma has taught you to say your prayers at night? Well, after you finish saying them, you can ask Jesus for what you want Him to do for you."

"You mean I can ask Him, and He will do it!" I thought for a few seconds then I came up with this bright conclusion, "Can I ask for a doll like Rita got?"

The Result of Teaching

Tee hee! Of course, she went on to explain to me how things worked with God. I got up from that little talk feeling as if I had been handed the most precious thing there was. It was like it was a special secret I could hug all to myself.

My mother started me on something she knew would carry me through my whole life, even after she was gone. She reminded me of this many years later, before she died. She reminded me that the Lord had been taking care of me all my life and that He would continue to do just that as long as I kept my hands in His hands.

Folks, I have just shared a moment in my life that my momma gave me that has lasted me my whole life long. She equipped me with what I needed so I could be strong, and I have shared it with you to reiterate the need for sharing things with our families and others. I am writing my story down because I remember how blessed I was in having the mother I had, in that she taught me so many values and principles from the laws of God. She taught me stories from the Bible, and she taught me by the way she handled her troubles. She taught me strength through her tears.

You might be saying, "That is a nice little story and all, but what does it have to do with us?" Good question, and I am glad you asked. I am passing forward to you what my mother taught me—Deuteronomy

9–10 KJV—as I reach another milestone in my life. I am using this opportunity to brag on God (Jeremiah 9:24 NKJ).

Why I Am Passing It Forward

During my years as a public educator, I saw children who did not know what it was to be raised with Godly values and principles. Remember how we talked about the influence and legacy we live and leave to our loved ones? Well, many children do not know the Godly thing to do, because they have never been taught. So I am writing these things down in this book to teach, inspire, motivate, and remind us of the awesome responsibility we have as standard setters for others. Though we are but pilgrims passing through, what we do in our tenure does matter, for it does affect others.

In lesson 10 we read the statement, "Use your talents to glorify Him." I believe, as I have told you before, in "Doing What I Can, While I Can." I was once asked to speak at a black-history program, and at the end of the speech, people were very complimentary. I thanked them all, and when some children came up to me later and wanted to meet me, I was a little shocked. After all, I am just "Mrs. Alma," or so I was called when I still taught in public schools. But one compliment stood out in my mind then and does today. There was a lady there that I admire, and she told me I needed to be doing public speaking as a second career, since I had retired from teaching. My mouth fell open. She then said, "Yes, that is exactly what I mean. People are making big bucks for what you just gave us." Then she said, "I am proud to know you!"

I realized then that I had been given an extraordinary gift, the gift of being an encouraging speaker and writer. That is why I am writing it down, folks. I told the Lord a long time ago that if I were on the top of the tallest mountain in the world, I would yell to the world of

His love for us and my love for Him. Ladies, that is what I am doing. I am shouting it from the tallest mountain in my world. I tell it to all who will listen. I tell it from my blog (viewed from several countries around the world) and from my five published books (published in several countries).

Let's Recap
What are we teaching by our lives?

1. When I look back over my life, I remember my charcoal-bucket days, and I am glad they are no more. I realize that God brought me through it all.
2. Am I teaching people to be strong during their stormy time, or am I teaching them, by example, to fall to pieces?
   * Childhood days—I lived in abject poverty, but I kept praying.
   * College days—There was not enough food to eat, few clothes, but I kept praying, and I kept going.
   * Barren days—Friends became mothers, but not me...I kept on going.
   * House-burning days—Despite great pain, I pushed on, even though I didn't understand.
   * Diabetic days—I persevered, kept praying, and kept believing.
   * Old-age days—Now I am telling my story and bringing God glory by writing it all down as a record for you and others who may follow.

Thank You

Thank You, Father, for people placed high and low
Who extended the hand of friendship to me
As my row, I continued to hoe.

Thank You for the people who did beneficent things to me
Even if, of their motives, I was not sure.
The end result was that a blessing I did receive.
Thank You, God, for my guardian angel,
Whose name I do not know,
But whose lovingkindness landed upon my heart
So many years ago.
Thank You for Jesus, Who brought me back to You.
Thank You for You, Lord, in all Your
Omnipotence for the things for me that You do.
Thank You for putting my pen to paper
So that some others can see and/or be reminded of Your glory.

§

Everybody's Children

For what it is worth,
Nurture, encourage, push, and prod.
Do this because we know that
Children are special
In the eyes of God.

§

Discussion Questions

1. Why is it important to write down encouragement and wise words?

_____

2. Does writing a religious book that is encouraging in its purpose compare to sites like ancestry.com? How?

_____

_____

3. Is leaving a favorite recipe just as important as leaving favorite prayers, etc.? Why?

FOR FURTHER READING
Deuteronomy 6:5, Isaiah 50:4 MSG

Answer the Roll One Day (2 Corinthians 5:9-10, Acts 17:31, Hebrews 9:27, Revelations 21:4 KJV)

§

AIM: To BE REMINDED TO keep doing our best to love our fellowman, because we will give an answer to the deeds done in this body. To emphasize that we are traveling through time on our way to eternity, where every tear will be wiped away, because trouble, heartache, etc. will not be allowed in heaven.

Song: "Going Up Yonder"/ "Heaven Is on the Other Side"

INTRODUCTION
Oftentimes, only "ultimately" pushes us onward.

What is your take on the above sentence? Take a moment and give it some thought. Okay, have you had an ample amount of time to ponder the italicized statement?

It conveys a popular sentiment that "The buck stops here." But if we give it a spiritual meaning, it could convey a message that means *everything*, and I do mean *everything*. Every good deed, every heartache, every disappointment, every smile, every betrayal, etc. stops with the Lord.

Case in Point 1—I knew better because experience told me
(Wedge Head)

My ears are very sensitive to blowing cold air or wind, and so I have to keep earmuffs on them when I am out in the wind. Well, I did not do that for two and a half days, and now I am paying the penalty for that. Yes, I have drainage from my ears, which in turn has given me a scratchy throat, which in turn makes me cough, which in turn makes my nose run, which in turn makes me feel a tad under the weather. Not to worry, though, for I will be taking some Claritin D and some cough syrup and should be good to go very soon!

I bet you are wondering, "What in the world is a 'wedge head'?" That is a term coined by my mother. She called us that when she tried to tell us something but we were pretty sure we had it figured out our own way. Needless to say, we didn't relish being called that, because it meant "Uh oh, not paying attention to Momma. Licks might be next!" That word got our attention immediately.

In the event that we did not listen but kept doing our thing, we might receive the back of Momma's hand. Then we sat around thinking, "I should have listened. Bet I will next time. I'm not getting any more licks." Well, life does us the same way at times. We learn by trial and error what works for us and why. We do the thing for so long, it becomes a ritual. Then one day, we overthink the process and figure that maybe this is not the right way to do something this time. What happens? We get whacked by the situation, and we say, "I knew better! Why did I ever think to change the way I always do things?" Have you ever had a situation like that? I'm pretty sure you have.

That is what happened to me yesterday. I took my cold medicine in the morning, and it lasted for about eight hours. Upon retiring for the night, I decided I did not need the night medicine. Needless to say, I awoke this morning more stopped up and congested. You know what I did this morning? Yep? You guessed it. I took that twelve-hour tablet and my cough medicine. Further, I will be taking that twelve-hour capsule tonight as well, as the instructions said. I learned my lesson!

Let's take my lesson and learn from it further. We have the Holy Writ, so we know what is coming down at the end of time. It behooves us not to be wedge heads and to try to carry out the Lord's commands down here now, because we will not have the opportunity to say, as I did with my cold medicine, "Oops! I knew better. I will do that next time," for alas, there will be no next time.

In essence, let us wrap our little selves in His love and make plans to meet Him in glory for a blessed reunion at the judgment, okay?

You see, one day the work of peacemakers and troublemakers will cease, and somebody will relate the news that we have found release from this earthly plane. There will be no need for peacemakers, because we will be residing with Jesus, the Prince of Peace. Troublemakers will be allowed to wreak havoc no more, and as I have said before, they and all their kin will not be allowed inside heaven's door!

It will be grand!

I got up before the chickens to get my Sunday dinner done. After worship, all I need to do is cook cornbread. A job satisfactorily done. That is what I want to hear at the end of my time here on earth when I stand before the Lord in the judgment: "Well done, Alma. Enter into the joys of the Lord." Won't that be a grand day, folks? But, until then, we will keep pressing forward as we work our way down the row we have been assigned to cultivate in the vineyard. And we will do it with joy, hmm?

Case in Point 2—Can't you just imagine when you have been hard ridden all the way to the other side and those old denizens think they can sail right through the city gates with you? Ha ha ha! I have told you before that I am a skipper, and that is true. What I am going to do is fall out laughing when trouble, heartache, disappointment, and all of the rest of that crowd are stopped cold at the gate. They cannot say, "We are with her." Ha ha ha! That won't wash, and I will lie down and howl with laughter, then I will hop up and do what I have told you I would do, start my skipping. I'm gonna skip high and skip long, if they let me. But I know I won't be the first one to go berserk with happiness, so they will all probably say something like, "It's okay; she just arrived from below."

Actually, I don't know how it will go, but I tell you this, whenever He wipes my final tears and turns me loose in the streets of glory, I will skip! It's as simple as that. And I just might howl with glee, too. One thing for sure, no matter what form it takes, I will rejoice! You too?

We are moving toward an ultimate destination. A date has been set on the other side of time. The title for this lesson is fitting, because it implies that nothing is over. It won't be over until the end of time. It reminds us that we must keep going, no matter the stormy sessions we have, and no matter the pain.

Look Down the Road

If you think that your life is rough,
Just look down the road.
Somebody else may be
Carrying a heavier load.

These are the words that I want to hear said:
"Well done, Alma, well done,"
For those old ladies that you

Helped to cross the street
And those little children whose
Tears you wiped from their eyes, etc.
My angels were the ones that you
Did those thoughtful things to.

Because of the adversary, it will get rough sometimes. Yet we must keep our hands in the faithful hands of the Lord. If we keep giving it our best, He will make everything all right. Keep going, soldiers; don't stop. Whether it is heartache, pain, sorrow, disappointment, grief, betrayal, etc., always remember that that burden cannot last always. It is but a page in the plan book of your life. Why do I say that? Well, think about it; from start to finish, your story was written before you were born! The ending has already been written. All you have to do, my friend, is stay the course, so keep blooming and sending up that sweet-smelling savor for the Lord. He will handle all else. That means, whichever comes first, judgment or change, we wait with assurance of our "ultimate" hope, Glory.

Here is a little poem I penned for you on the subject.

Tinkling Slivers

The ground cries with tinkling slivers,
And if you are among will make you shiver
The God who can do such pretty things as this makes me
Wonder what other awe-inspiring joys He will deliver?

The tinkling slivers are a reference to something known as needle ice that comes up from the ground and makes a tinkling sound as it creeps along on the ground. I learned about this on the Weather Channel, and I was simply amazed. I briefly wondered what it would feel like to sit among the crawling slivers and have them grow around me a bit. Then common sense told me that it would be a novel experience but a cold one! Still, I would like to experience it if I could. Why? Just because! You must remember, if I had been with the Israelites as they fled Pharaoh and crossed the Red Sea, I would've been the one to rake her hand through the wall of water. I am also the one who, as a child, stuck a pin in a socket to see what it would do. Just curious, I guess. I was a bit of a hot mess as a child, and I am so glad He kept me safe. I sometimes wonder if He doesn't put a special detachment of angels with me because He knows how I get to wondering about things. (By the way, there is a YouTube video on Needle Ice. You will enjoy it!)

I can be awed by things I see and/or experience, and I have a very fanciful imagination to take my mind further. I cannot even begin to conceive of joys that go beyond that, joys that He has prepared for us. But that is the way that it is! Y'all, it is going to be wonderful! So very wonderful, and I get to go there to stay...

I wanted to paint you a poetic picture of my imagined joy when I get home, so I attempted to do it through these poems of mine, especially this first one, which has become one of my favorites. I just wanted to give us all some additional stamina for those times when life gets in the way. Enjoy the painting I tried to paint as you waltz through difficult times.

Heading for That Rise

I'm on my way home with joy in my step.
I'm getting closer to my journey's end;
It's the thought of heaven that has always kept
Me plodding on through many a storm and contrary wind.

Joy quickens my soul; I'm headed for that rise,
For when I get to the top of the mountain
I'm headed to a meeting in the skies.

You can't stop me now; I'm on the run.
My struggles are just about over,
And my race is just about run.

It was hard scaling valleys and climbing high mountains,
But hallelujah, folks, I can see the waters
Of that great crystal fountain.

All I have to do is climb this last hill, and them I'm home.
Glory to GOD, folks, the Angels are coming to meet me
To show me that I'm not alone.
Move over, enemy; you can't stop me now
I see the wonders of Glory
And all I can say is, "**W.O.W.!**"
(Excerpt from *W.O.W. created w.o.w.*)

§

Ere we get there
What's it going to be like—
A city so bright and fair
Can't wait for what's fixed for you and me
Don't you, too, want to see?

§

Care not what you think of me.
Long since relinquished that chore.
Striding on to what He would have me be
As I make my trek toward eternity.

§

RIVER of LIFE

The river of life keeps flowing along,
Through good times, bad times, through right and wrong;
I don't understand all of life's ups and downs,
I just keep plodding on, in hopes of a crown.

I've shed some tears, endured some pain,
Had time in the sunshine and time in the rain;
I smile when I can and cry when I must,
But in the GOD of heaven, I put all my trust.

So when my earthly sojourn comes to an end,
And the river of life flows around that final bend;
I pray sweet guidance to my eternal home above,
Where I can rest from my labor in peace, joy and love.
(excerpt from DEI Sub Numine Viget, *Under God's Spirit, She Flourishes*)

Another Day's Journey

Another day's journey and I'm thankful and glad.
Sometimes I think about the myriad of other days
That I have already had; did I do good things or did
I do things that could be deemed as bad?

Then I remember that it does not matter
What I did before,
Because the blood of my Savior
Has already evened the score.

Be blessed, and happy Saturday everyone,
And remember to BYDWP,

Because you will need a Friend
When time gives way to eternity.

§

Dried Her Tears

That will be a great day
For us Christians, one and all,
For if we have remained faithful,
We will eagerly await the roll call.

Yes, the best is yet to come,
Just you wait and see.
There will be untold joy
If we stay faithful 'til eternity.

As I have told you before,
I am going to be beside myself
When I get through heaven's door.

I had a lady in the hospital
Giggling quite a bit
When I stood around her bedside
And told her what I would do
Once I got inside.

Y'all know that I have told you
That I have always been a skipper,
And when I described my joy to her,
I told her I would be quite the quipper.

I told her that in my mind's eye
I could see old trouble and old pain

Peeping through the gates of heaven
Itching to, but not able to get at me.

I told her that if I had arms, hands,
Legs and feet, in a body of some kind,
That I would lie down on the ground
And with glee, my fists I would pound
The turf while pointing and laughing with glee
At old trouble and old pain, saying,
"I'm rid of y'all for eternity."

She snickered in earnest then, and gone
Were the tears that she had had in her
Eyes when first she called me near
And asked me if for her I would pray.
I'm glad she beckoned to me from her bed.
I'm glad that she felt better for something I said,
But how could I not try to lighten her load
When she, bless her heart, was such a dear?

No, I am not a comedian, just a child
Who is willing to do all that I can to
Help fellow travelers as we make
Our way back to our homeland.

For one day, He will make the final choice,
And we, dear friends, will get the chance
To shout with jubilant voice
Along with the angels as we all rejoice.

I am thankful to be given one more day for building for Him as He
prepares a home for me. When I get there, I can enjoy the things He
has prepared that cannot enter my mind and my heart yet because
they surpass my understanding. Don't you know that nothing this

life has thrown at us will matter then? Ah, in the hands of my Jesus, that will be enough for me. Ahh, how sweet it is, and how sweet it will be!

DISCUSSION QUESTIONS
1. Explain Revelation 21:14 KJV in reference to us today.

_____

2. What is the occasion for joy in the poem? For laughter?

_____

3. How does the green highlighted word in the poem describe the way we should act regarding our work and love for the Lord?

_____

_____

4. How will you feel after hearing the Lord say, "Well done"?

_____

FURTHER READING
Matthew 12:36; Revelation 20:11–15; John 12:48; 2 Peter 3:10–13; Matthew 25:36–40 KJV

LESSON 13

Lest We Forget: New Kid on the Block
(2 Timothy 4:2-5, 1 Timothy 5:18 KJV)

§

AIM: TO LEARN TO BE mindful of preachers and their wives as they work in the garden for the Lord.

Song: "May the Work I've Done Speak for Me"

Introduction: Make their work not hard, for they watch after your souls

All of us are given
Different tasks to perform
What's routine for me
May not even be your norm.

But you know, folks,
I learned a long time ago
Not to judge another
For the work done in his shoes,
Because I might do similar or worse
If for the task, me, He decided to choose.
(Let's be mindful of our treatment of all who watch for our souls.)

New Kid on the Block —For the Sister Who Is New to Being a Preacher's Wife

As I told you in lesson 10, I was not ready to be a preacher's wife when my husband first started preaching. Listen a bit as I tell you a portion of my first taste of being a preacher's wife.

I remember when my husband was first asked to be the minister of a small congregation, I was ready and prepared—at least I thought I was. Little did I know. Let me tell you: I did not know people could be so mean and so negative about anything and everything, or that they could be so unreasonable. When some of those ladies at the new church got through with me, I felt just like a plucked chicken who had been nipped, scratched, and clawed so much that I felt I did not have another feather of goodwill left in me. When I got home I prayed about it, and the next week, the same thing happened. I was upset enough that I was almost sneering and wanted to tell somebody, anybody, "Who does she think she is?" But I didn't; I got into the car instead and waited for my husband. That was a joke. He turned out to be no help, because he had a bigger problem that needed to be worked out before Sunday.

I was on my own, but thank God for Godly elderly sisters. I lived next door to one, and when she asked me how things were going for us at the new church, I broke down crying. She let me have a good ol' cry, and then she told me to get a tissue and dry my nose. When I got my nose all wiped, she looked at me with a piercing gaze and asked me if I had prayed about it. I don't know what it is about some elderly sisters, but they can pin you with a look that seems to go clear to your soul. I told her that yes, I had prayed. She told me that maybe I had not prayed enough. I thought to myself, "You don't know; it's not you they are picking on." She told me that as a preacher's wife, I was going to have to pray more than I ever had in my life. She told me, "I know you think you have been praying before, but it is like your husband is a general in the army now, and you have to do your part as a helpmeet. You can't go running to him with every little thing, because the work of the whole church rests on his shoulders." She told me I was going to have to help him carry the load.

That is when I came out with my pet answer, "I don't know why he had to become a preacher. He wunn't no preacher when I married him! And, and (sniff) anyway, if I had wanted a preacher, I would have married one. (Sniff, sniff) The old me would have told them a thing or two!"

She raised up in that chair, slightly pinned me with a glacial glare, and said, "Now you listen to me, little miss preacher's wife. YOU ARE MARRIED TO A GENERAL IN GOD'S ARMY NOW, AND WE DON'T DO THINGS THAT WAY! 'Vengeance is mine I will repay' is what the Lord said in Romans 12:19 KJV. You just go on and pray to the Lord. You *will* be all right!"

I don't know what it was about her words, but they gave me comfort, and armed with the Lord, I went boldly on. Those words carried me on when folks got upset:

* whenever I got a new pair of shoes or a new dress
* when I refused to listen to gossip about someone
* when I would not laugh at dirty jokes
* when I moved into a new house or got a new car or paid my offering, etc.

I learned not to get upset by the things that anyone did, pretty much. But during those times that they did manage to get to me, I prayed until:

* I learned to control my face and put on a poker face so you could not tell what I was thinking.
* I learned not to resent the fact that the members expected me to be a miniature preacher and, since I was married to the

preacher, be able to tell where certain scriptures were found almost as well as he could.

* I learned not to resent the fact that they expected me to be more holy than most other members.
* I learned that I was a trendsetter, so I learned not to wear my dresses too short.
* I learned that whatever hairstyle I adopted, several other ladies would adopt that same style.
* I learned that everybody was not my friend, and I learned to talk to only God about most things.

> **Prayer**: *It is my prayer that you not be troubled in mind by rude and seemingly heartless people, but that you be able to shrug off their rudeness like water runs off a duck's back and see a possible soul for Jesus.*

Case in Point—There was a young lady who was considering leaving her place of worship because she had become so disheartened and so hurt by the callous and manipulative people she encountered. She was a new preacher's wife and had not expected church groups to be like that at all. I counseled her briefly and left the above prayer with her. I told her I had learned this prayer when my position as a minister's wife was new to me. I told her I found it handy then and still find it handy today because, though names and faces change, there will always be someone who wants to take a bite out of you.

If you pray that prayer, I believe you will be able to feel pity for people who act as I just described. You might even chuckle to yourself a bit after they see that you are not bothered anymore by their shenanigans. Just remember to thank the Lord for your ability to shake it off. Yes, I know that people who are supposed to be His ought not to act like that, but remember in 2 Timothy 4:2–5 KJV, we are told to endure hardship. It tells you that the life of a preacher gets rough at times. We have to remember that He said an enemy has sown tares among the wheat and that He, Our Father, will do the separating at the end of time (Matthew 13:25–39 KJV). How can I say this? It comes from being a preacher's wife for forty years. Let me tell you that I had to learn to give it all to my Father. And that, baby, is how I made it this far and am making it today: trusting in the love that the Lord has for me—and you can, too.

New to Being a Preacher's Wife

To the wife of a husband
Who has just started preaching,
Living under a microscope is
Not really that bad.
You assess the situation
And look at the former occupant of the position,
Then you get in and do your best
To upgrade the job's condition.

To be effective you must
Get used to praying like
You have never prayed before
And having your every look,
Gesture, reaction, and expression
Read and interpreted
Like an open book.

You will get used to it after a while
And can even bear the scrutinizing
With a soldier's smile.

For you are a leader in the army now,
And your ways are no longer your own.
Everything has to be thought out
Before you make a move,

Because, even at the best of times
Someone less seasoned will pick apart
Whatever you say or start.

Carry on, soldier who just
Moved up in the ranks.
Get your praying armor on
To be prepared for the enemies' tanks.

A lot you will learn by
Trial and error, for sure,
But that is the mark
Of a true Christian soldier—
The ability to endure.

To the Ladies of a Church Where There Is a New Preacher's Wife

Give her a break; she is
New at this job or task.
Be lenient in your criticism
Is one thing I would ask.

You think her green about the gills,
And while that may be true,
Somebody fed and nurtured you
Through your new days of
Learning your job's skills
So, give the preacher's wife a break
As she dons her new mantle,
And her new helpmeet's arsenal
She learns how to build.

1. Explain 1 Timothy 5:18 KJV.

   _____

   _____

2. Why should the world treat its preachers better than the church does? To get to be head cheerleader, you must always be willing to put the needs of the squad ahead of your own. Can you apply this principle to life? Our preachers are like our quarterbacks. Since we realize the load that they carry, we should cut them some slack. You would appreciate the slack cutting if you were in their shoes. Who knows? Someday you may be.

FURTHER READING
Matthew 28:18, Acts 8:4, Romans 10:14–15, Isaiah 52:7 KJV

Storm survivor, what is your Case in Point (your story), and are you telling it?

WORKS CITED

The Bible. Scripture taken from *The Message*. Copyright © 1993, 1994, 1995, 1996, 2000, 2001, 2002. Used by permission of NavPress Publishing Group.

The Bible, King James Version. Nashville: Holman Bible Publishers, 2000.

The Bible, New American Standard Version. Indianapolis: B. B. Kirkbride Bible Co., Inc., 1993. Print.

Deen, Edith. *All of the Women of the Bible*. New York: Harper & Row Publishers, Inc., 1955.

Franklin, Kirk. "Lean On Me." https://play.google.com/music/preview/T7iesw7fp6wwndwhakjnqez7jae?lyrics=1&utm_source=google&utm_medium=search&utm_campaign=lyrics&pcampaignid=kp-lyrics

Sorgum Halepense: Johnson Grass. 2 June 2004. <http://www.texasinvasives.org/plant_data/detail.php?symbol=SOHA

Other Works by Alma L. Jones
AVIA (poetry)
DEI Sub Numine Viget (poetry)
W.O.W. created w.o.w (inspirational poetry)
Tallest Mountain in My World (inspirational blog book)